"Haunted Southern Nights®"

Volume 3

History

and

Haunting

of the

Mentone Area

Written by:

Deborah Collard, RN

Haunted Southern Nights®
Volume 3 – History and Haunting of the Mentone Area

Copyright © 2008 by Deborah Collard
Haunted Southern Nights®
ISBN# 978-0-578-00990-2

All rights reserved. No part of this book may be reproduced or utilized in any form or by any means: electronic or mechanical, including photocopying, recoding, or by any information storage or retrieval systems, without permission in writing from the publisher. For more information contact:

Deborah Collard at nealparasociety@aol.com

Printed in the United States of America
Cover Design by Deborah Collard
Photo taken by Deborah Collard at DeSoto Falls

Acknowledgements

"Haunted Southern Nights®" lives on in Volume 3, Haunted Mentone. I want to thank so many special people in my life that have wished for me nothing but the best life has to offer. My family first and foremost including my husband Greg, my Mom, Barresa and Ricci, my daughters and the love of my life, my granddaughter Kaylee Ann.

I want to thank the Town of Mentone and the citizens of Look Out Mountain for being so gracious as to offer to me their friendship and the Bruce family heirs for allowing me a home that I can call my own in beautiful Mentone, Alabama. I offer a special thank you to my Sisters of the Mountain Gloria Sitz and Cynthia Stinson the Innkeepers of the famous Mentone Inn. Also a special thanks to Andy Talton of the Mentone Springs Hotel. For those I miss, thank you!

For all of my friends who have given me such heart felt encouragement through some rough times this year and leading me onward to believe in myself and the power of our God and Creator of this wonderful earth that I continue to grow with my writing and teaching others about a topic I love, the spiritual world.

A special note of thanks to Robert Atchley for hanging with me through this long ride, I love you just like my own child.

Many blessings to all of you,
Deborah

Table of Contents

1. The Mentone Springs – The Water of Life

2. Granny Dollar and Her Ghostly Dog Buster

3. The "Wee People"

4. The Mysterious Prince Madoc

5. The Sallie Howard Chapel

6. Battelle – A Ghost Town

7. Little River Canyon Speaks

8. The Mentone Springs Hotel

9. The Mentone Inn

10. Graham Manor

11. The Hitching Post

12. The Camps

Introduction

As I have nested into mine and Greg's new vacation home in Mentone I have felt the forces much larger than man permeate into my being. I have sat with the spirits that linger here on the mountain, I have sang with the angels that watch over those who reside here and I have wept with the earth as how I fear that a place so sacred could ever have a modernization take control of it.

There is no "time" in Mentone. Each day begins with light and ends with darkness. Even through the darkness the heavens are so very close you can near reach them with one hand.

As I look down to the ground I see fallen leaves of a season in passing, as I look ahead I see the beauty of a neighbors smile, as I look above I see God's face smiling down on me.

This book has been a personal joy to compile. I have connected myself with distant relatives, age old spirits and ancestors who will never be forgotten.

Enjoy the journey with me and I promise we will take one again very soon.

~Lovingly
Deborah

The Mentone Springs
"The Water of Life"

Photo Owned and Courtesy of "ItmakesCynts"

This is now all that remains of the once infamous Mentone Springs. The Mentone Springs that have been in existence for years no longer run due to the error of man there is only a trickle of water now unfortunately. There were actually two springs in Mentone. The second spring, "Beauty Springs" is owned by Alex and Honey Glover.

Back many years ago when Highway 117 was being built there was blasting done on the side of the mountain. The best we know is that during this blasting a shift of the surface of the ground and its underlying sandstone crimped the black iron pipe used for the water to run was crushed leaving the springs to run no more.

The Mentone Springs owned by Dr. Frank J. Caldwell was used as a "healing springs". Dr. Caldwell came to Mentone at first as a boarder in the house of the John Mason family following his first wife's death and during that time he built the "Mineral Springs Hotel". Dr. Caldwell felt strongly about the use of these "healing springs" as he felt their result as had John Mason who is considered the founder of Mentone.

In later years when the hotel was purchased by Charles Loring, the springs name changed again and they became "Loring Springs". Given a name by those who adored the springs allows us to take a look at what mystical power do mineral springs bring and what spiritual energies remain. To understand the whys and how one is has to understand what exactly a "mineral spring" is.

Mineral springs have been used for healing for centuries therefore we can safely assume that our Native American brothers and sisters used these springs for a similar purpose. In fact to Native Americans, as I am one, treat these springs as sacred and with deep respect emotionally, spiritually and physically as well as the surrounding land. To our people these sacred springs were a place of great peace, given honor by all tribes whether they are at war or not.

Modern society would tend to consider these springs a more romantic location rather than what they had to offer in the past to those who were ill and afflicted by disease. We who are still mystified with the past and naturally attuned to nature find much more than romance there. We find ourselves wrapped up in the history of the springs and wandering through time to envision the beauty it once beheld along with all those before us who have enjoyed its blessed healing. Maybe that is one reason why some spirits remain near the Mentone Springs.

The Mentone Springs began with a reaction from the earth, a gravitational reaction. An artesian aquifer is a confined aquifer that contains groundwater that will flow upwards out of a well without the need for pumping. An aquifer provides the water for an artesian well. An aquifer is a layer of soft rock, like limestone or sandstone, which absorbs water from an inlet path. Porous stone is crushed between impermeable rocks or clay. This keeping the pressure high, so that when the water finds a hole or outlet, it overcomes gravity and goes up instead of down.

So why did so many people gather around the Mentone Springs? Was it from the religious aspect? All the way from the Garden of Eden in Genesis to the sacred lands of Jerusalem, holy lands have had a deep impact on cultural life. The beliefs associated with such lands have literally created volumes in the history books which in turn have significantly forever altered our perspectives on life. Such areas even that of the "Mentone Springs" with its healing properties takes on a religious aspect.

What do we find with the scientific aspect? Humanity a product of natural evolution has always been dependent upon the forces of nature whether they are good or bad for the support of "life". Such locations as the "Mentone Springs" was prized by various cultures and by examination of its history we find contained rare elements in its natural environment that are conducive to human development and healing.

For example the story of the native New Yorker, John Mason, Founded Mentone after coming to Lookout Mountain about 1872 in search of pure mountain air and mineral water to restore his failing health.

Mason had gone to the West early in his life and later settled on a farm in Iowa and made his fortune. But his health began to decline at the age of fifty and he began searching for a climate that could restore him to a healthy state.

During his search he was given a glowing account of Lookout Mountain's healthful atmosphere. So Mason made his way to the mountain and, after residing with a family who lived above Valley Head, Alabama for several months, his health grew much better.

He returned to Iowa, but soon he became ill again and determined to return to Lookout Mountain to settle permanently. Mason loaded his family on a steamboat for Memphis, and then traveled by rail to Chattanooga.

However, the Alabama Great Southern trains were not operating at this time due to an epidemic. The intrepid Mason loaded his family into a wagon and struck out through Lookout Valley.

He settled at a site on the mountain above Valley Head and remained for the rest of his life, enjoying the benefits of the pure mountain air and the mineral water. He lived to be almost ninety-two years old.

I believe it to be a simple answer. In most all cultures, mineral springs have had large traditions in healing. The use of water for healing is an art as well as a science. Hydrotherapy is the application of water in any form whether it be used externally or taken internally in the treatment of disease and the maintenance of good health. Hydropathy refers to the "water cure" which began from the empirical tradition and the profession that water could cure all diseases, especially cold water. As we know Mentone Springs was a cold water spring. Crenology or crenotherapy is the science and use of the waters such as Mentone Springs.

Mineral springs can be used in four major ways to assist in healing: bathing, drinking, medical application and inhalation. You ask me to explain. Bathing is the most popular form and involves immersion for whatever time one desires. Bathing removes dirt, germs and revitalizes our bodies. Medical application includes using the mineral water cold or hot as water packs, cleansing of wounds or dilution for medications.

Drinking mineral water which has become commonplace in the retail market for giving back to our bodies and allowing our body to cleanse itself internally. Remember the human body is primarily made up of water; therefore we must consume much to remain hydrated. Inhalations of water vapors are used to help people with asthma, sinus problems, allergies and other respiratory problems.

Let us look at the contents of a geological study of the water of the Mentone Springs to aid us in understanding how this "miracle" springs is just that! The analysis I found was done by a Mr. Hodges from the springs at Mentone in Section 28, Township 5, and Range 10 E. when owned by the Loring Springs Hotel Company.

	Parts per million
Potassium	1.3
Sodium	2.6
Magnesium	3.0
Calcium	4.5
Iron	6.5
Alumina	2.3
Chlorine	.8
Sulphuric acid	15.4
Carbonic acid	33.2
Silica	10.8

While meandering around the Mentone Springs direction I noticed many locations that appeared to have been graves. Most likely Native American since they had been covered with rock. That is normally how they were covered. That in itself tells me that the Mentone Springs and the land that surrounds it would be sacred.

We pray that someday someone will take what effort is needed to revitalize the "springs" and allow them to flow freely again through the shrine that was built so ornately around the head flow.

Do you know the history of the beautiful shrine? One can only speculate but do so with grandeur as we look back in time when "mineral springs" were considered "holy water". The egg shaped formation built around the spring could be considered a guardian. As reputed in folklore as being the entrance to other worlds this would be one idea or a pilgrimage, a place where rituals would be carried out prior to healing with those secret details hidden from us or a gathering place of a social sort.

This spring was indeed a holy place and its future is dim as the flow is nil. We have this spring here in Mentone; adopt it, whether you visit it once a year or once a season, bring to it your hopes of a bright future.

With that being said there are tales of a young man and woman all dressed in white that their spirits can be seen on some foggy nights near the Mentone Springs. Are they newly weds? Are they just enraptured by the Mentone Springs believing that if it will run again they can regain 'life'? But as it is they remain together even in death. So what do the Mentone Springs have to do with this couple? Could it be the place they first spoke words of love to each other? Could it be where they vowed to remain?

What a place in history these two have selected. There would be no better choice on earth than the infamous Mentone Springs.

The Legend of Granny Dollar

Nancy Callahan Dollar B. June 27, 1826 – D. January 20, 1931

Granny Dollar was born Nancy Emmaline Callahan Dollar, in or about June 27, 1826, the daughter of William Callahan and Mary Sexton. William was a full blooded Cherokee Indian with a hot temper but when it came to family a very loving man. Mary, on the other hand was mixed blood, her mother being Cherokee and her father, Irish. It's easy to see how Granny Dollar had the 'spunk' her legends pass on to us.

Nancy "Granny" Dollar was born to be a mother but she never bore children in her 100 plus years on this earth. Instead she became the mother to her other twenty-five siblings. You wonder how? Well it appears that her father William not only had his family here in Alabama, but also another family with an Indian wife in South Carolina. Let me share some of the details passed down.

William and Mary Callahan lived in Buck's Pocket, now an Alabama State Park located in portions of Marshall, DeKalb and Jackson Counties. Buck's Pocket is a two thousand acre park that the Cherokee people once lived prior to and during the Trail of Tears. Also something many aren't aware of it that in the 1700's the French that settled there grew coffee and olives. What brought the Callahan family to Buck's Pocket was the hard drive, the force of the Native Americans that had to walk the Trail of Tears. William and his family hid out in a cave in Buck's Pocket and were able to stay there long enough for all the soldiers to pass and settle there. The area was plentiful in wildlife, land that would grow good crops of vegetables and of course water, a river full of it.

As the story goes after an afternoon hunt, William came in with a big deer. This deer was enough to feed a very large family but William couldn't eat a bite of it.

When Mary asked William why he could not eat he explained that he had another family in South Carolina and he didn't know if they had food. She was surely amazed as he told her he had three children there, two boys and a girl, also another wife. Mary being the caring woman she was told him to go get them and bring them home. She knew in her heart there was enough food for all.

It was not uncommon and was accepted for Indian men to have more than one wife during this time. So off William went and gathered up his other family and returned with them to Buck's Pocket.

From all the stories told both of the wives got along fine and before all was said and done the family grew hardily to total twenty-six children. It is said that Mary, Nancy's mother gave birth to three sets of triplets. It is unknown if all three sets lived.

The Callahan family was set until William found himself in an encounter with a particular local by the name of "Jukes" in what began as a cuss fight and concluded with William having bitten off one of Jukes ears and his nose. This began an uprooting for the family and William moved them onward because he was afraid that someone would attempt to harm his family so they moved to Marthasville, what we would now call Atlanta.

At twenty one years of age Nancy Callahan had to find a means to help support her family. At this point in time we find that one of the mothers is dead therefore her strength is tested in filling the shoes as the other mother of this large family. This remarkable young woman would begin the path of a provider by taking on the job of hauling goods from her home in Marthasville to country stores as far out as thirty miles.

How she managed, I have no clue but this woman who was tall and had her father's stature and evidently the will and strength of two would drive a wagon with the tar poles and canvas to cover the goods leading two mules with blinders to each of the stores to bring in much needed supplies to the masses of settlers. Nancy had slaves who helped her to load the wagon full of cases of molasses, meats, salt, and dishes for the home. Also things that were much needed by the settlers like powder, lead, gun caps and wagon wheels. Not to mention hand made shoes for children and adults alike.

When Nancy arrived at the general stores the shop keeps were more than happy to help Nancy unload. It is said that Nancy would keep doing this for some twenty years of her life and during that time she was never robbed or being a woman, molested by anyone. That is remarkable in itself her being a woman.

One of her regular store owners had a son, Thomas Porter. She had talked to Thomas on more than one occasion and they became engaged over time. Unfortunately Nancy would not know wedded bliss at this time due to the fact that the Civil War came about. Thomas joined the Confederate Army and was killed during battle. To add to her loss, her father William who also had joined was killed too in The Battle of Atlanta.

In one of Nancy's interviews that I've read she said that she would never forget the sound of the battle fire in Atlanta. I don't believe I would either. That day she took responsibility to many other fatherless children to ensure they did not go hungry. She continued her path as a provider and with that she dictated the respect of many and many more as they read of her today. Nancy lived on and was single for another forty plus years.

Something special happened to Nancy when she was in her sixties. Nancy met a man, Nelson Dollar, who would make her life more full. She had many years before raised her siblings, most of them dead by this time but she still had remained a single woman.

When Nancy married Mr. Nelson Dollar it was one of the best days in her life. Nancy and her new husband moved to Mentone where they were very happy. Twenty years later her husband died. But Nancy being the kind of woman she was sold a head of livestock and paid for a tombstone for her late husband.

After Mr. Dollar passed, Granny continued on with her daily routine. It is said that she told people's fortune. She was evidently a very "sensitive or psychic" person indeed. She also did the basic farming to raise money and keep herself fed by growing chickens and vegetables and by the kindness of her neighbors and friends. It is said that Granny Dollar just loved to tell stories and loved even more knowing that they were being repeated to others about her trials, tribulations and triumphs of her life.

She spent the remaining six years of her life in the old cabin that belonged to Colonel Milford Howard. There are still some ruins of her home place in DeKalb County near DeSoto State Park.

Colonel Howard who was an author among other things wrote a story about her and it was published in the Birmingham News. Colonel Howard was indeed responsible for continuing with the increasing interest in the legend of Granny Dollar. As a woman, she was immortalized by many. In trade for Granny watching over things Colonel Howard supplied Granny with some fat back, tobacco for her corn cob pipe and feed for her chickens and her famous dog "Buster".

Buster was Granny's dog, her everlasting companion in both life and death. Buster was said to be twenty years old when Granny died. Buster was the one witness to all of Granny's doings, from telling stories about the past to chasing chickens to being a mid wife. Buster loved his master.

One day in 1928 the word began to spread that Granny Dollar had died. Some believed her to be one hundred one years old, but no one really knew for certain. She was so rambunctious, who could know? But one thing was for sure, she planned. She even planned for her own death. Granny managed to save twenty-three dollars for a tombstone but someone stole it from her and her neighbors who watched over her as she had watched over them took care of her funeral expenses. The Colonel gave her eulogy.

Buster grieved and grieved. He would not let anyone near him. Oh how he missed Granny Dollar, his master. No one wanted to take him for fear he would bite them or even a child. So Buster was put down with chloroform and laid to rest right next to Granny Dollar. The Colonel did another funeral, this time for Buster. Both Granny Dollar and Buster are buried at Little River Baptist on Lookout Mountain.

This author has personally viewed the Alabama Health Department Burial Certificate for Nancy Emmaline Callahan Dollar. The document states that the county of interment is DeKalb, the city of River Park. It further states that she was 105 years of age and is referred to as a "white female". Application of permit and listed as Undertaker the signature of M. W. Milford and that she was buried on January 21st, 1931 in Little River Church graveyard. Notes on the document state that she was born eight miles from Coffee Town, Alabama and also that Nelson Dollar had died four years prior to her death.

It is said the spirits of both Granny Dollar and her faithful companion in life and death Buster wander about the woods off DeKalb County Highway 156 on the south side of the road only a short distance from Mentone and the DeSoto State Park where Granny's home once was. They say Granny's spirit is still angry that someone stole her burial money and she wanders about in search of them.

Since 1973 when her grave marker was placed they say that she has calmed down a bit and doesn't show herself as often. Sightings of Buster have continued on since his death. He's happy now so he moves about the woods knowing that his master is very close by. So if by chance you see an old woman with a dog walking along the road late at night on a County Road in Mentone, don't think twice. Just smile and know the Legend of Granny Dollar and her infamous dog Buster lives on.

The "Wee People"

There was once a woman of Mentone, Alabama who had no belief in the "Wee People" although the stories of them fell true to many. This particular story has been passed down. This woman, we will call her JoAnne came to live in Mentone following the untimely death of her husband.

You see, Mentone is filled with vacation homes and that has been how it's been for over a century. JoAnne came here seeking to be in the place of some of her fondest memories of her life with her husband as they owned a vacation cabin here. JoAnne was not sixty yet so she was still very young, both in body and heart.

As JoAnne settled in she decided that as spring was approaching she, who had been raised on a farm having a family vegetable garden decided to plant one of her own and did so with much success.

JoAnne noticed as the garden was "coming in" some of her vegetables like tomatoes, carrots and other things came up missing. This was after spying a tomato and deciding to give it another day to ripen before picking. The next day it was gone! So as any of us would think maybe a small animal got it.

Well JoAnne decided to put up a small fence around her garden as it was time for many vegetables to "come in" and she did want to lose her entire crop.

JoAnne monitored the garden and noticed a carrot had been pulled up from the ground. "Well", she thought! How could that happen? So JoAnne with more than enough time on her hands sat and watched very early several mornings while having coffee in a row only to get the shock of her life. Rocks were placed on one side of the fence and then on the other side like "steps". Ok, this was getting a little odd to her. So, she took the steps down. Well that didn't work for the next morning they were back again and more vegetables were missing! "Oh my" she thought.

JoAnne decided to stay up all night on lookout for whatever or whoever was stealing from her. And then she saw them, "Wee People", a fairy like little person come into her garden area, go over the rocks, get a carrot and back over again and disappear into the rocks in an abandoned lot next door!

So at that moment in time, filled with shock and amazement she thought the stories were fact, not fiction. She had always heard that when the soldiers came back during the Trail of Tears when they were rounding up all the Indians, gathering them up in families to take them to the encampment in Fort Payne that something had happened.

The "Wee People" were friends to the Cherokee. So when they came for this family the "wee people" set the soldiers pants on fire as they walked across the rocks and ran those soldiers off and the Cherokee family had ample time to get away from them. The Cherokee were friends to the "Wee People" and those stories go back for many centuries.

JoAnne started taking out to the steps going into the garden little bits of bread and leftovers she had. They would be gone the next day. Then she began to notice little things, helpful things, around the yard had been taking place. JoAnne knew she had made friends with the "Wee People".

This went on for many years until JoAnne got very sick. Her daughter Anne came to take care of her. JoAnne would tell her daughter to take food to the fence. Anne thought her mother's fevers had driven her to madness but under the circumstances did as her mother asked. Ann then had to sit with her mother as her time came close.

JoAnne's final words were "I love you Anne and you must take care and feed the "Wee People" for they are your friend, not your enemy.

These words were taken in heed to and following her mother's death two nights later, overcome with grief, Anne goes out to take some extra food that was left from all that the neighbors had brought and as she sat and wept near the rocks out came the "Wee People".

Anne sat there through her tears and found happiness, for her mother was not "mad", she was telling her the truth. Anne smiled and said "thank you" to the "Wee People" for being there and told them "my mother loved you". The "Wee People" walked away. Anne came back to Mentone to settle in her mother's cottage as that it was her home now. To this day she feeds the "Wee People" who are not ghostly images but little people whose mystery will never be solved but their stories will go on forever.

History excerpt from Native American Lore on the Wee People from Stones Web Lodge 1996 StoneE Productions

The Little People of the Cherokee are a race of Spirits who live in rock caves on the mountain side. They are little fellows and ladies reaching almost to your knees. They are well shaped and handsome, and their hair so long it almost touches the ground. They are very helpful, kind-hearted, and great wonder workers. They love music and spend most of their time drumming, singing, and dancing. They have a very gentle nature, but do not like to be disturbed.

Sometimes their drums are heard in lonely places in the mountains, but it is not safe to follow it, for they do not like to be disturbed at home, and they will throw a spell over the stranger so that he is bewildered and loses his way, and even if he does at last get back to the settlement he is like one dazed ever after. Sometimes, also, they come near a house at night and the people inside hear them talking, but they must not go out, and in the morning they find the corn gathered or the field cleared as if a whole force of men had been at work. If anyone should go out to watch, he would die.

When a hunter finds anything in the woods, such as a knife or a trinket, he must say, 'Little People, I would like to take this' because it may belong to them, and if he does not ask their permission they will throw stones at him as he goes home.

Some Little People are black, some are white and some are golden like the Cherokee. Sometimes they speak in

Cherokee, but at other times they speak their own 'Indian' language. Some call them "Brownies".

Little people are here to teach lessons about living in harmony with nature and with others. There are three kinds of Little People: The Laurel People, the Rock People, and the Dogwood People.

The Rock People are the mean ones who practice "getting even" who steal children and the like. But they are like this because their space has been invaded.

The Laurel People play tricks and are generally mischievous. When you find children laughing in their sleep - the Laurel People are humorous and enjoy sharing joy with others.

Then there are the Dogwood People who are good and take care of people.

The lessons taught by the Little People are clear. The Rock People teach us that if you do things to other people out of meanness or intentionally, it will come back on you. We must always respect other people's limits and boundaries. The Laurel People teach us that we shouldn't take the world too seriously, and we must always have joy and share that joy with others. The lessons of the Dogwood People are simple - if you do something for someone, do it out of goodness of your heart. Don't do it to have people obligated to you or for personal gain.

In Cherokee beliefs, many stories contain references to beings called the Little People. These people are supposed to be small mythical characters, and in different beliefs they serve different purposes.

"There are a lot of stories and legends about the Little People. You can see the people out in the forest. They can talk and they look a lot like Indian people except they're only about two feet high, sometimes they're smaller. Now the Little People can be very helpful, and they can also play tricks on us, too. And at one time there was a boy. This boy never wanted to grow up. In fact, he told everyone that so much that they called him "Forever Boy" because he never wanted to be grown. When his friends would sit around and talk about: 'Oh when I get to be a man, and when I get to be grown I'm going to be this and I'm going to go here and be this,' he'd just go off and play by himself.

He didn't even want to hear it, because he never wanted to grow up. Finally his father got real tired of this, and he said,' Forever Boy, I will never call you that again. From now on you're going to learn to be a man, you're going to take responsibility for yourself, and you're going to stop playing all day long. You have to learn these things. Starting tomorrow you're going to go to your uncle's, and he's going to teach you everything that you are going to need to know.' Forever Boy was broken hearted at what his father told him, but he could not stand the thought of growing up. He went out to the river and he cried.

He cried so hard that he didn't see his animal friends gather around him. And they were trying to tell him something, and they were trying to make him feel better, and finally he thought he understood them say, 'Come here tomorrow, come here early.' Well, he thought they just wanted to say goodbye to him. And he drug his feet going home. He couldn't even sleep he was so upset. The next morning he went out early, as he had promised, to meet his friends. And he was so sad; he could not bear the thought of telling them goodbye forever. Finally he began to get the sense that they were trying to tell him something else, and that is to look behind him.

As he looked behind him, there they were, all the Little People. And they were smiling at him and laughing and running to hug him. And they said, 'Forever Boy you do not have to grow up. You can stay with us forever. You can come and be one of us and you will never have to grow up...we will ask the Creator to send a vision to your parents and let them know that you are safe and you are doing what you need to do.' Forever Boy thought about it for a long time. But that is what he decided he needed to do, and he went with the Little People.

And even today when you are out in the woods and you see something, and you look and it is not what you really thought it was, or if you are fishing and you feel something on the end of your line, and you think it is the biggest trout ever, and you pull it in, and all it is a stick that got tangled on your hook, that is what the Little People are doing. They are playing tricks on you so you will laugh and keep young in your heart. That is the spirit of Little People, and Forever Boy, to keep us young in our hearts."

The Mystery of Prince Madoc And the Welsh Caves

The mystery of the various legends of Prince Madoc have brought questions to mind as to who actually discovered America. I'm not sure that we will ever know the truth but if we could have been flies on the wall back in 1170 A.D. we certainly would have an idea.

You wonder what this has to do with haunting. Well from time to time you can hear odd noises coming from the area of those caves: the beating of drums, laughter and screams and why is that?

Was this an area of encampment with a history of savage behavior or an area where attack was eminent at any given time?

We will discuss the various fortresses that surrounded this alluring monument of a mountaintop cave and why this was such a good hiding place for such an illustrious and powerful man if only for a temporary time.

Prince Madoc was said to be the son of Owen Gwynedd the Prince of North Wales. Madoc's exploration adventures have been noted in various documents requested by Queen Elizabeth I who was an English Queen of Welsh lineage. There was a document in support of a proposal to solve the problem of English Catholics by 'evacuating' them across the Atlantic, prepared by Sir George Peckham and addressed to Queen Elizabeth, carried a preface dated 12 November, 1583, which stated:

'And it is very evident that the planting there shall in time right amplie enlarge her Majesties Territories and Dominions (or I might rather say) restore to her Highnesse aunciant right and interest in those Countries,

into the which a noble and woorthy personage, lyneally descended from the blood royall, borne in Wales, named Madock ap Owen Gwyneth, departing from the coast of England, about the yeere of our Lord God 1170 arrived and there planted himselfe, and his Colonies, and afterward appeareth in an auncient Welch Chronicle, where he then gave to certaine Llandes, Beastes, and Fowles, sundrie Welch names, as the Lland of Pengwyn, which yet to this day beareth the same.'

The earliest known account in print of the story of Madoc came from David Powel's 'The Historie of Cambria' published in 1584:

'Madoc ... left the land in contention betwixt his bretheren and prepared certain shipps with men and munitions and sought adventures by seas, sailing west ... he came to land unknown where he saw manie strange things ... Of the viage and return of this Madoc there be manie fables faimed ... And after he had returned home, and declared the pleasant and fruitfulle countries that he had seen without inhabitants, and upon the contrarie part, for what barren and wilde ground his bretheren and nepheues did murther one another, he prepared a number of shipps, and got with him such men and women as were desirous to live in quietnesse, and taking leave of his freends tooke his journie thitherward againe ... This Madoc arriving in the countrie, into which he came in the yeare 1170, left most of his people there, and returning back for more of his own nation, aquaintance, and friends, to inhabit that fayre and large countrie, went thither again.'

Now the story of Madoc guides us to the history of the Mandan Indians. The Mandan Indians who eventually moved from the area of Mentone, some believe, to upper Missouri from being overrun by the Cherokee. This was Cherokee country back then no doubt about it. In comes a white man with supposedly about two hundred men and women. To some historians it is estimated that only 5% of these Welsh people survived and intermarried with the Mandans. The connection to the simple ways of life of the Welsh in comparison with the Mandans makes us more intrigued. The Mandan Indians lived in round, earth habitats very similar to those found in Wales. Another very difficult to believe similarity was the boat structure. Of course there is the infusion of red and blonde hair, blue and green eyes and the fact that Mandan's understood the language of the Welsh and used it at times.

Charles Michael Boland wrote a book called "They All Discovered America". In his book he references the battle between Madoc's clan and the Cherokee at the fall on the Ohio. A truce was called and Madoc agreed to leave the area.

This information tends to contribute to the factuality of our Southern man, John Sevier's letter which is now lost to all that explained the battle at a river falls but he says it's in the Muscle Shoals on the Tennessee River. This battle was similar to the above battle but there is some history afterwards. It is said that buried beneath the mud in this battle location were exhumed several bodies that were wearing brass plated shields bearing a mermaid and a harp which is indeed a symbol of Wales. Notwithstanding was a stone excavated that read the date 1186. So were some of Madoc's scouts trekking a path from Little River to the Tennessee River and looking for areas to settle? These people seemed to always be following a water path which also would be significant.

There are several forts, such as Fort Morgan in Georgia that were laid out in Welsh fashion. There is also one in Mentone and another in Tennessee. Could the falls Sevier was referring to be DeSoto Falls? And the river is Little River? No one will know since the letter has been LOST! The cliff that leads up to the Welsh caves appears to have been carved with some type of pre-Columbian tools of sorts. The Welsh caves consist of four compartments or rooms. One would appear to have been for cooking and keeping a fire going, another for resting, and another for lookout and another for gathering. I say it's very interesting and should have more study done. As agricultural proof I have read that a tree was cut down in 1819 and had three hundred thirty seven rings, and it was a seed tree so that would date it to 1482 but the fort at the base of the cliff had been built many years prior. So the mystery deepens.

If Prince Madoc was the first visitor to come to America he could not have found a better location than that of the Mentone area. We'll continue to listen for the sounds that come from the Welsh caves to see if we can find residual spirits that continue to inhabit the area.

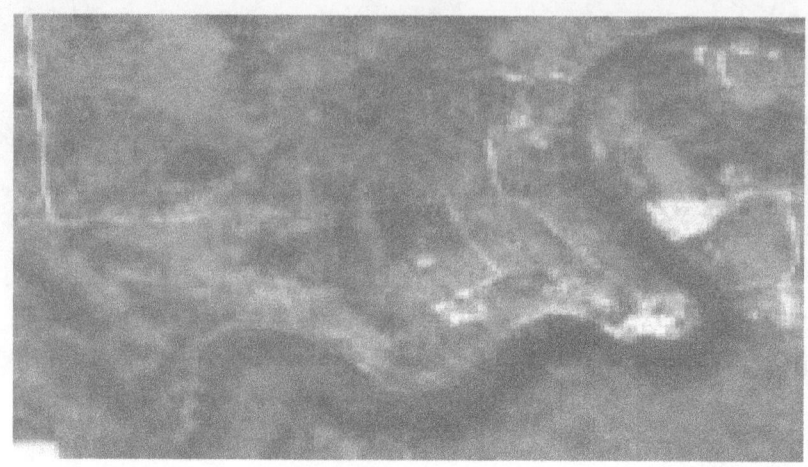

What appears to be the boundary wall of Madoc's territory?

View from high atop that reveals the possibility of a fortress.

Mandan village…..what is different about this structure based on Native American structures of early American? This is much more advanced and has some Welsh commonalities.

Let's over-view some facts to determine for ourselves. Was Christopher Columbus actually the first to discover America in 1492 or by Prince Madoc Abbywaine Gwynedd of Wales in 1170? History is for the most part this day and time delivered to us in a compilation formed by genealogists who gather familial information. Not to say, that history has been documented forever by genealogist, but historical documentation has come from the oddest mean. Hieroglyphics on the walls of caves, rocks arranged in unfamiliar manners, is another way it's been done is writings on scrolls. But those who know the land have studied the land are rarely historians. Let's look at the facts now:

FACT 1. In 1170 AD., a Welch Prince by the name of Madoc sailed from Wales which at the time war filled and poor. He took his ships but his direction to west and headed that way. He came back to Wales speaking of a new land, he spoke so highly of it that many of his people crossed the sea with him to go back.

FACT 2. The land that was wonderful is thought to be that of Mobile Bay in Alabama. For over 5 Centuries there have been reports of white Indians who could speak Welch.

FACT 3. Madoc was one of 17 sons; the earliest printed account is from Dr. David Powell's "The History of Cambria" published in 1584.

"Madoc...left the land in contention betwixt his brethern and prepared certain ships with men and munitions and sought adventures by seas, sailing west...he came to a land unknown where he saw many strange things...Of the viage and returne of this Madoc there be many fables faimed, as the common people do use in distance of place and length of time, rather to augment than diminish; but sure it is that there be was... And after he had returned home, and declared the pleasant and fruitfulle countries that he had seen without inhabitants and upon the contrarie part, for what barren and Wilde ground his brethern and nephews did murther one another, he prepared a number of shipps, and got with him such men and women's were desirous to live in quietnesse, and taking leave of his freends tooke his journie thitherward againe...This Madoc arriving in the countrie, into which he came in the yeare 1170, left most of his people there, and returning back for more of his own nation, acquaintance, and friends, to inhabit that fayre and large countrie, went thither againe."

FACT 4. Other documentation that validates Madoc:

A. A Brief Description of The Whole World in 1620 by Sir Thomas Herbert, B; De Originibus Americanis in 1652 by Horuins, a Dutch writer, and c; Principal Navigations 1600 by Richard Hakluyt. Gutyn Owen, Welch Historian and Genealogist, negates that others say the Madoc Story was told after 1492 so that Great Britain could claim power and ownership of the new world. His writings not only include the Alabama-Florida region but also West Indies and Mexico, although the Mobile Bay theory is felt to be the true landing.

FACT 5. It makes sense that the ocean currents would carry Madoc into the Gulf of Mexico. I mean after all Ponce De Leon, Alonzo De Pineda, Hernando DeSoto, and Amerigo Vespucci accessed the harbor in Mobile Bay by following the Gulf currents.

FACT 6. There are a series of Pre-Columbian Forts that were built along the Alabama River and the words spoken by the elders of the Cherokee of the White People who built them. In proof there is a letter dated 1810 from Gov. John Sevier who was responding to a question by Major Amos Stoddert Note: *A copy is on file at the Georgia Historical Commission.* This letter goes over a discussion Gov. Sevier had in 1782 with Oconosoto the 90 year old chief of the Cherokee Nation. When Chief Oconosoto was asked by Gov. Sevier about the white people who left the fortifications Chief Oconosoto replied, "The were a people called Welsh and they had crossed the great water. He called their leader "Modok", Chief Oconosoto stated "It is handed down by the fore-fathers that the works had been made that formerly inhabited the country" Chief Oconosoto said he had heard his father and Grand father say they were a people called Welsh and they had crossed the great Water and first landed near the mouth of the Alabama River near Mobile.

FACT 7. There are three of these fortresses; they are not of Indian origin. Archeologists have testified it has been stated that the forts are of Pre-Columbian origin, and most believe they pre-date 1492. All the fortresses are felt to have been built during the same time frame and are similar to those fortifications built in the same time frame as Wales. The first fort we find **here** near DeSoto Falls this fortress is said to be almost identical in setting, design, and means of construction, to the birth place of Prince Madoc. The Dolwyddelan Castle in Gwynedd the fortresses coincide with the accounts given by the local Indians that one can follow the colonization of Madoc's trail.

The Indians forced Madoc's people up so they built Fort Mountain in Georgia that was 3000 up and the main defensive wall 855 feet long. Then as they left and started farther north into the Chattanooga area they built some minor fortifications, and then they built their final fort called Old Stone Fort on the forks of the Duck River in Manchester, Tennessee. The Old Stone Fort spread 50 acres; it was formed by high bluffs and had 20 foot walls of stone, and a moat that extended protection 1200 feet around. Chief Oconosoto has gone farther in his recollections and noted the whites followed the Tennessee River up to the Ohio, then up the Missouri, and said their were no more white people they are now all Indians.

There has been tremendous evidence based on Chief Oconosoto testimony that those who met these Indians that lived up on the Missouri not only claimed to be ancestors of the Welch but could speak the language.

So to my readers you have to understand that I'm not asking anyone history, because fact of the matter is they won't. Columbus Day comes once a year for it is a holiday, but should it be Madoc's day. Do we have the proof right here near Mentone, Alabama, of the true discoverer of this great land? I hope this gets someone's attention, I hope we have a young group of archeologists who are intrigued enough to seek the truth and prove for once and for all did Columbus or did a Welch Prince by the name of Madoc?

The Sallie Howard Chapel

The Sallie Howard Chapel is a Memorial to the beloved wife Milford Wriarson Howard. Milford Howard was born Dec. 18, 1862 the son of Steven Oliver and Martha Maddry Howard in Floyd County, Georgia. Milford traveled to Fort Payne, Alabama on Nov. 7, 1880 to begin practicing law in the office of Col. L.A. Dobbs.

Milford applied at age 19 on Jan. 1881 for admission to the Alabama State Bar. Milford Wriarson Howard was one of the youngest men ever admitted to the bar.

Milford was noted for being a dreamer and he pursued his dreams with such courage. Until he either attained his goal or suffered loss. He but his total being into any project he set his mind to.

He wasn't a small man in fact he stood 6'4. He was healthy man, a gentle giant, with tenacity that ran deeply as he was a brilliant man. Who could remember a person five years ago down to the color of the suit they were wearing. Milford was so comfortable in the speaking forum that he would recite quotation from famous writers, experimentalist, or even entire chapters of the bible.

Even though Milford was so talented he never quite seemed fulfilled. He held so many jobs during his life that it amazes this writer how he could not see his successes.

Milford was not only a lawyer; he also did the following jobs: Farmer, Congressmen, Educator, Lecturer, Author, Actor, Newspaper Writer, Real Estate Dealer, Newspaper Editor, Cattle Breeder, Mine Speculator, Oil Speculator, Gold Prospector, and even the Owner of a Salmon Canning

Factory in Alaska. Some of Milford's aggressiveness to achieve so much was related to being born to an over bearing father who dominated his wife and seeking to work for his money and stay out of the home.

His family lived in poverty with no pleasures or entertainment. He had little or no opportunity for schooling for by the time he was 14 years old he had only attended school six months.

In all his spare time Milford would read and when he was 17 he did get to go back to school. A brief term of three months and he had to walk three miles barefoot just to go. And then at 18 years old with less than a year's formal schooling he went to Major Joseph A. Blange in Cedartown, GA.

The attorney was shocked that Milford would ask him to let him study law under him. He advised him to just forget it but as we know Milford's aggression got his dream fulfilled. When he came to Fort Payne he only had the clothes on his pack, a nap sack with only a few personal items which included $30 and most precious possession his bible.

Col. L.A. Dobbs traded with Milford. Milford had to keep fire in the fire place, and the office cleaned and he could use the Colonel's books. Along came a beautiful 15 year old blonde haired, brown eyed girl by the name of Sallie Lankford. Their romance continued and they were married Dec. 2, 1883. Milford and Sallie had three sons Clyde, Clarence, and Claude. Clarence unfortunately died at age of 11 months.

Before he was 30 he took his first step in to politics as chairmen of the Democratic executive committee of DeKalb County. He actually organized the first Democratic Primary ever in DeKalb County. Gov. Thomas Seay took note and appointed Milford the first county attorney of DeKalb County. Milford even though at the hype of his law career became interested and studied speech and drama in Washington DC. He had recently lost a fortune during the Fort Payne boom period and he found excitement in the audiences that he could grope their attention. When he got through with his lecture tour he wrote book on corruption and scandal and titled "If Christ Came to Congress" published in 1894.

During this same year Milford became the congressmen for the seventh district. When returning to Fort Payne he bought a local newspaper of which he was the editor, feature, and short story writer.

When his wife and children became dormant working on the farm and pleaded to go back to the city Milford moved them to Birmingham and practiced law for a couple of years. Due to some unforeseen illness he stopped practicing law again and speculated in Mexican mine, Louisiana Oil Field, moved to Alaska for Gold Prospected and ended up building a Salmon Cannery.

To have so much brilliance and integrity a showcase of a man he still was plagued by the fact that no matter what he did he was still losing money. So once again came home to Fort Payne.

Howard took another quick move to California this time, but it took him no time to return to Alabama in 1923 where he started a school. The school was a major achievement in personal valor as much as it was for the poor children on Lookout Mountain.

The site chosen consisted of 1,000 acres of absolute wilderness. Mind you because he didn't have a lot of cash this purchase was made on credit, on his name. July 23, 1923 was remarkable day when the four corners of the little school house were marked. The school house was built of native stone it had two dormitories, and a dining hall. School started in the fall of 1923 with about 40 boys and girls enrolled.

Milford had hoped to receive donations and contributions for the school until it could stand on it's own but as luck would have it there was very little of that. So he decided to sell lots he would call this development Little River Park. There was an auction but it was unsuccessful. Milford got a $10 donation and started the building of a dam to improve Little River Park's value.

The construction was supervised by Joe Biddle who was former British Sailor. Along with Mr. Biddle the volunteers who helped build the school built the dam. It would not stop here because of the beauty the Milford saw from the bluff overlooking the dam, Alpine Lodge would be his next project.

He got deeper in debt but sweet Sallie his wife who was still in California would send him her money to help him out.

Sallie came to visit and spend the summer of 1925 while already in her last stages of cancer. She died almost immediately after returning to Los Angeles in fall.

It took Milford a while but he recovered from the loss of Sallie and his dreams and visions again returned. A scenic highway from Gadsden to Chattanooga would boost these 1,000 acres he owned and surely his property would sell then. A year following the death of Sallie on Nov. 9, 1926 Milford married Stella Vivian Harper.

No matter what he had done he could still not realize his dream. He began to meditate and write in his mountain top cabin while Vivian stayed away visiting friend and relatives. He thought often of Sallie, she was buried at Forest Long Cemetery in Glendale, California where the chapel Kirk O' The Heather which was a reproduction of the Annie Laurel Church in Scotland shook Milford to his very soul with its beauty.

He had desired deeply to build a church like that here on his mountain top as a memorial for his beloved wife Sallie. With his health failing he would not see this dream not come to fruition. He would not stop until he saw this dream come a reality. He supervised the construction of her memorial for months on in.

He had the help of the civilian corps boys and local businesses to help him. As you look up in to the rafters the words "God Has Always Been as Good to Me as I Would Let Him Be". Visitors may not be aware of this but that was in Sallie's last letter to Milford. Another rafter has a word that Milford believed so deeply in inscribed "Immortality".

During the summer following the dedication of the chapel June 23, 1937 Milford himself spoke a few sermons and as you can expect they were all on "Immortality".

Milford was gravely ill and took the train to California where he died Dec. 28, 1937 at 75 years old. His body was cremated. "Lady" Vivian held a private ceremony in the fall of 1938 where Milford's remains were interred inside the huge rock behind the pulpit. A bronze plaque is placed over it inscribed "Milford W. Howard Born Dec.18, 1862 Died Dec.28, 1937 "I shall Dwell in the house of the Lord Forever"".

After years of hearing the stories of how Sallie remains at the chapel with Milford and their spirits live as one in immortality. Stories of sightings of apparition of a Golden-Haired Petite lady in a flowing white gown and a tall man whose spirits still reside at the chapel.

This paranormal investigator decided to go to the chapel herself. As I opened the door and went in the hair on my arms stood straight up. There is such energy inside that beautiful chapel that I felt overwhelmed but it was not an overwhelming fear I felt. It was the over whelming feeling of a dream that had finally been fulfilled.

The dreamer Milford Howard had without mistake had accomplished his last dream in the most satisfying way possible. If asked do I believe that the spirits of Milford and Sallie are still in the chapel I would respond with a resounding yes.

When I left the chapel I began taking photos outside. There

were images of many faces looking out the windows. Whether they were matrixing or apparitions does not matter to me. Because I could feel eyes looking upon me not to instill fear only curiosity and gratitude that I had visited The Sallie Howard Memorial Chapel.

Bronze memorial *inside the Sallie Howard Chapel where remains of Milford are placed.*

Battelle
A Ghost Town

Battelle is simply a Ghost Town now in DeKalb County, Alabama. Battelle was at one time a thriving mining community which spread in a north-south line along the foothills of Lookout Mountain a mere five miles north of

Valley Head, Alabama.

The town of Battelle was named after Col. John Gordon Battelle. John Battelle had been contacted by mining prospectors who found pockets of good grade iron ore, coal and limestone. These were all the ingredients needed for making pig iron. The Lookout Mountain Iron Company was consequently formed by a group of Ohio mining speculators headed by Col. John Gordon Battelle.

Even though John had large investments in the iron and steel industries in Ohio and even the Middle West, he took such a large personal interest in the operation to which he had given his name. John Battelle actually moved here and personally oversaw the mine activities until unfortunately the mineral deposits were found to be of insufficient quality or quantity to compete with the mines farther south. In the south the Birmingham mines were producing large quantities of the necessary ingredients and were now being processed at the now famous Sloss Furnace.

When looking at the land where the community of Battelle once existed using your imagination you can visualize the workers and families sitting on their porches of once were over 100 homes.

In the main portion of the town there set a school, a company store, a hotel, and even a post office with Post Master Hawkins. Battelle had a towering furnace and multiple coke ovens. Battelle also had its own water system; water flowed from a spring running off Lookout Mountain near Mentone and was pumped into a large wooden tank and then piped into all the surrounding homes.

The families of Battelle enjoyed the closeness of a tight-nit working community. Many a child was born there, attended school and lived happily. But tragedy did occur at Battelle one fateful day; a worker named Drew Hester was at the top of an eighty-five foot furnace and fell tragically from the stack into the molted iron. Legends grew even up to this day it's believed that on nights when the moon bright Drew Hester's screams as he falls into the fallen molten iron can still be heard. His screams are so intense that they break all boundaries of forest sounds as the residual spirit relives the horrible fiery death. Even today paranormal investigators and curious ones attempt to debunk by walking five miles into these ruins to see if the spirit of Drew really exist in the ruins of Battelle.

When mining operations were stopped in Battelle they better homes were sold and moved the Ghost Town created, a lumber company called Belcher that was of Centerville operated up until the 1940's. This author found it amazing how many people she talked with have never even heard of the 1900's boom of Battelle.

Tragedy struck again in the Ghost Town of Battelle, in 1969 when the Alabama Great Southern Train left the tracks and propane tanks exploded. The news accounts stated that the wreck site was Battelle. Remains of Battelle are little to none the large furnace was purchased by the British Government during WWI. The furnace was then dismantled and shipped around the world to Calcutta, India. Although the city's founder financial expenditures in his namesake Battelle proved unsuccessful he had done very well with other investments. He died in 1918 John Gordon Battelle was a pioneer of the steel industry and former owner of

Columbus Iron and Steele Co.

Battelle's mother Annie Maude Norton Battelle was a suffragette. She married Battelle's father in Memphis, Tennessee in 1881 and moved to Ohio and lived in both the cities of Cincinnati and Pique before finally settling in Columbus in 1905. Annie Maud Norton Battle died in March 1929.

As the only son of John and Annie Battelle Gordon was trained and managed his father's holdings in the steel industry and left four million dollars to his only son John Gordon. Young Battelle attended military school in Chester, Pennsylvania and later studied metallurgy at the Sheffield Scientific School of Yale University.

Before having to take over his fathers business the young Battelle went out on his own and invested in lead mining and smelting operations in Joplin, Missouri. While in Joplin he became friends with a scientist George Waring who was working on a project to develop a process of recovery of commercial value of the tailings in mine water. Young Battelle was so intrigued he built a small lab for Waring which resulted in a successful completion of the process. From this experience Battelle gained tremendous respect for research for solving industrial problems.

He spent almost a year of his life visiting Laboratories all over the country to develop a plan that would integrate science and industry to bring forth opportunities and benefits to mankind. His impact on science and industry due to his belief that scientific research was not only means to make industry more efficient but it also indeed helped with solving social problems and bringing more esteem to the common man.

Battelle established the institute "For the purpose of education in connection with and the encouragement of creative and research work. And the making of discoveries and inventions in connection of metallurgy of Coal, Iron, Steele, Zinc, and their allied industries".

The younger Battelle unfortunately died in 1923 just five years later with appendicitis. John who already had a will left the remaining fortune to form the *Battelle Memorial Institute* in Columbus, Ohio.

The Battelle Memorial Institute is a private not for profit applied science and technology development company. The company traces it's origins of the 1923 Will of industrialist of John Gordon Battelle who provided for its formation. The institute actually opened in 1929 the institute initially focused on contract research and development work in the area of metal and material science.

Since then it has expanded the scope to defense, energy, environmental, transportation, and health and life sciences. Today it is the world's largest independent consulting, research and development organization. Battelle has played major roles in the development of projects including Xerox Process, Snopake Correction Fluid, Universal Code, and Compact Disc Storage.

Battelle who had developed a strong sense of social responsibility from his loving parents believed the way to achieve lasting impact and benefit from his wealth was to set up the Institute. The Battelle Memorial Institute donates 20% of its net income to the communities in which it works. These grants have supported many types of social, human and artistic cause but have mainly focused on math and science initiatives.

Today unknown to most local residents of Valley Head and Mentone the Battelle Memorial Institute conducts research in the areas such as global climate change, sustainable energy, technology, high performance materials, next generation healthcare diagnostics and therapeutics, and advanced security solutions for people in infrastructure, and the nation. They also helped develop commercial products to help fight diabetes, cancer, and heart disease.

This was totally unknown by this author but in the early steel industry Battelle was involved in "The Manhattan Project" which resulted in developing the Atomic Bomb in WWII this was the beginning of the institutes work in Nuclear Research. The Institute is probably best known for its invention and development "Xerography."

But let's not leave the mother of Battelle for she was very well known for being one of most formidable social matriarchs.

Memories of the once thriving community of Battelle still live on today.

You wonder how, this author has visited several residences with very well known local Charles Bain who was kind enough to show me the results brick remains from Battelle that had been used to establish family homes in the Mentone and Valley Head areas.

Indeed Battelle maybe a Ghost Town with a legend of a haunting but Battelle is a very fond memory to the residents of Northern DeKalb County. I feel that I have been blessed by being able to share this knowledge of Battelle and all that as evolved from this remarkable family of Battelle's who thought so much to name the community after themselves that their spirits of giving, sharing, and loving still remain.

Colonel John Gordon Battelle

A picture of a furnace at that time. Courtesy of Gloria Sitz. This is her Mother and Aunt in the above photograph.

Gordon Battelle

Coke Ovens that remain at Battelle

The Tipple at Battelle

Numbered Battelle Bricks

Little River Canyon
The History and Mystery

The Little River Falls

LookOut Mountain and Sand Mountain have been stated to have been formed in the Pennsylvanian epoch some two hundred ninety to three hundred twenty million years ago. To those of us who do not understand the term "epoch" let us look at the definition possibilities.

1. a defining moment in the beginning of, or characteristic of, a distinctive historical period or era.
2. a criteria, a type of time division of the geologic scale based on rock layering which is less than a era (geology), age (geology), and period (geology) while being greater than an stage. (Geology also uses other spans not found in similar language contexts)
3. a phase in the development of the universe with distinctive properties during the the "Big Bang".

This statement gives us an idea of the magnificence of Little River Canyon. Both LookOut Mountain and Sand Mountain are simply foot plateaus at points reaching two thousand feet and above then nestled deeply within LookOut Mountain a trailing gorge that drops six hundred feet deep you find this beautiful and relentless trail that can at times so mercy to its visitors and sometimes no mercy to those who don't respect its challenges.

Let us begin when Little River Canyon was called May's Gulf. Many people don't even know this story as brief as it is. The Civil War began in 1861 and ended as we know in 1865. During the Civil War one of the more dramatic episodes occurred during Streight's Radio that occurred in neighboring Cherokee County. There is an historic trail that runs sixty-seven miles from the Coosa River Valley that recognizes the actions John Wisdom know as "Citizen-Soldier".

Wisdom rode from Gadsden to Rome, Georgia to warn citizens of the coming Union raid. Streight was pursued by Confederate General Nathan Bl. Forrest and was forced to surrender sixteen hundred troops to a smaller force of six hundred soldiers on May 3, 1863, near the town of Cedar Bluff.

Following this even within the same year prior to the Chickamauga Battle Union General Rosecrans's army were ordered to cross LookOut Mountain to attempt to cut off Braxton Bragg's army to stop the supply feeds to Atlanta.

This brings us to earlier times during the Civil War when battles had occurred along the Canyon rim in 1864. A Union General by the name of Andrew May was leading his troops east across north Alabama to meet up with General William Sherman who at that time was gathering a large that was going to make that famous march across Georgia.; May's trooops were being closed in on by the Confederate Army. When General May and his troops were crossing over LookOut Mountain they encountered the mighty River Canyon. The troops could not find a way to cross! There, on that ridge Confederate troops were able to close in on the

Union soldiers. When General May, who survived this event wrote his report of the battle he took it upon himself to name this might River Canyon, May's Gulf.

The Canyon was still to see Civil War action. After the 1864 Atlanta battle in which General Sherman claimed victory, he skirmished with the Hood troops across Little River. Following this Sherman arrived in Gaylesville on October 21, 1864. Sherman reported that he had about 60,000 troops in the Little River area. His forces withdrew from the Little River area on or about October 29, 1864. It is though that this is where he finalized his march that would lead him to Savannah, Georgia.

During this time it is noted that there were residences that spread along the rims of May's Gulf (Little River Canyon). The types of housing were log cabins which were associated with the yeoman farmers with the central hallway or as we call it "dogtrot".

It is believed that the oldest home in the Little River community of Shinbone Valley is the one called Daniel-Tucker. It is also said that this one and a half story dogtrot served as the headquarters for Confederate General Hood in 1864. The house is near Little River Canyon Mouth Park. There were grist mills and sawmills about, as that was the local industry associated with that time frame of the Valley.

Then came the "Boom Days" in DeKalb County as Battelle was one of those communities. Railroad lines were needed to transport the products. Railroad lines were being built that connected LookOut Mountain ore mines to ship to valley furnaces. This railroad line was then known as the Tennessee, Alabama and Georgia Rail Line. That is where we get T.A.G., now kept in the thoughts of Mentonians through the T.A.G. Blues Society founded by Gloria Sitz, Innkeeper of the Mentone Inn and more commonly known as "Memphis Annie".

TAG was originally the Chattanooga Southern Railroad that served Georgia in 1887 and then into Alabama in 1890. When the line was being surveyed for it to run through Shinbone Valley in 1890, Colonel Woolsey Finnell visited the May's Gulf (Little River Canyon) and has been quoted as saying, " Why go to Colorado to see the Royal Gorge. Little River Gorge is much longer, more rugged than and almost as deep as the Royal Gorge.

It is far more scenic."The railroad was run about a mile from the south end of the gorge. Back in the day this route was called "Pigeon Mountain Route". They advertised the railway using a photo of a pigeon flying across the mouth of the ***tunnel*** going through the Pigeon Mountain in Georgia. The route was indeed very scenic as it ran the length of LookOut Mountain from Chattanooga, Tennessee, to Gadsden, Alabama, then in 1911 it was renamed Tennessee, Alabama and Georgia Railway.

The North Tunnel Portal

South Tunnel Portal and Water tank

This water tank survived into Southern Railway ownership.

By the 1950's the TAG Rail had discontinued its passenger service and operated a gasoline motor car called the 'scooter" to haul passengers and mail. By 1971 TAG was sold to Southern Railway System and parts of it were abandoned by the 80's. During the "heyday" of the TAG railway people enjoyed the scenic views of Little River Canyon.

It's so fascinating how a river could flow for almost its entire length down the idle of our LookOut Mountain. Over many centuries the river has carved out the Southeast's deepest canyon, a natural wonder.

During the era of President Roosevelt he developed a "New Deal" that provided a plan for developing the economic potential for North Alabama among other areas. The Tennessee Valley Authority, Works Progress Administration and Farm Security Administration were the Federal programs that resulted under the "New Deal". The National Park Service and the Civilian Conservation Corps began to cooperate with Alabama to develop May's Gulf in 1933. Civilian Conservation Corps camps were built in Fort Payne. They were near the Edna Hill Church and Little River close to the G. Euclid Hill home.

In 1934, Alabama established DeSoto State Park on Little River in DeKalb County. In 1937 a decision was made by the Alabama State Commission of Forestry and the Nation Park Service to have DeSoto Sate Park and May's Gulf combined into one large state park. But they had one problem. The problem was that Alabama Power held the title to the land along the river between the two tracts of land.

In 1939, again the Alabama Power Company was asked about acquiring the additional land for DeSoto State Park. In a statement made by the Director of the Alabama Department of Conservation he described May's Gulf as "and ideal spot for the production and maintenance of desirable wildlife species and is widely known for its scenic beauty. The area could become a Mecca for lovers of nature". He also stated that it would be a good opportunity to build nature trails, bridle paths and much more while the Civilian Conservation Corps boys were available.

In 1939 it happened, they were combined but there was still the question of the land owned by Alabama Power. The park at that time was supervised by Frank Berry, the brother of Martha Berry, educator and founder of Berry College, resident of Mentone who had donated land for the park.

This brings up the "changing of the names" timeframe. I've noted that it was done on the recommendation of a special board by the Department of the Interior and the other was that in 1953 the residents of Fort Payne and Centre voted to change the name of Mays Gulf to Little River Canyon. Either way it became "Little River Canyon".

The following photo postcard belonging to Harriet Pentz was in her collection from the early years of this area.

A dedication ceremony finally took place in June of 1954 of a 16 mile paved road that was built along the rim of the canyon, to get the park recognized and some publicity flowing its way. G. Euclid Hill, the County Commissioner and Chairman of the 'Board of Revenue worked arduously for 30 years to see this recognition come to fruition. The location chosen for the dedication was Eberhart Point.

In 1967 the State of Alabama and the Alabama Power Company, after all these years, entered into an agreement for a cooperative wildlife management and public hunting area.

The State of Alabama leased 10,000 acres of land from Alabama Power Company for one dollar per year.

On February 9, 1995, the Department of the Interior, National Park Service purchased the upper portion of the Upland Forest Unit and Little River Falls from Alabama Power Company.

Canyon Mouth Park was donated by Cherokee County Alabama in 1996. In 1997 the National Park Service accepted another 1619 acres inside the boundary of the Preserve. That land includes all of Little River Canyon itself.

Little River Canyon has long been noted as an area with natural and cultural resources. Little River is also noted for its almost completely unpolluted and pristine condition as it flows through five impoundments.

The next photo shows how the water even when dry fills deep water holes. Some of these holes are extremely deep and dangerous.

Little River is unique in many ways but one that is simply remarkable since it is the only river that forms and flows almost its entire length on the top of a mountain. Because there are no dams to regulate its flow and very few pollutants this river close to home is one of the cleanest and wildest waterways in the South.

The towering cliffs are a challenge to any rock climber, the rapids when they flow indeed are intimidating to the experienced kayaker, the wildlife a vision to behold and foliage that is so dense it breeds a new life into the words oxygenated air. I've heard people say that they actually become dizzy from breathing such pure air? I say its doing your lungs a service just being here.

The drive along the twenty three mile scenic view is wonderful no matter what time of year you choose to do it.

It's hard to believe but at some locations in this massive piece of God's masterpiece the water is six hundred feet deep! Little River Canyon is a paradise for many forms of wildlife and plant life, some that are endangered…some that serve as mysteries.

Our Little River Canyon has been referred to as "The Grand Canyon of the East" and as I look down into it I can understand where this statement could be taken as very accurate.

Now lets get to how on earth this majestic location could have haunting and things that go 'bump' in the night. Well here come some of the legends, lore and stories told for fact by locals.

At one location within the park there is a church, only the ruins remain. It is said that on various nights that teens over the years and adults alike have heard voices coming from the church, voices loud enough that the visitors could not get out of there fast enough in their vehicles. Could these be residual entities? That has yet to be seen.

I have been personally told a story of two men who were in a particular area of the canyon, actually on a fishing trip. Both men were sober, ok! They smelled an awful smell and heard sounds that made their skin crawl. They both dropped their fishing poles and began to ascend the mountain path they had taken down. When they got back to the top then they had the nerve to turn around and look back.

What they saw they will never forget. Large human/animal like figures: Sasquatch or Bigfoot. They know and have respected that area for years. Neither discuss this publicly nor will they disclose the location but from what this author was told there were numerous amounts of them and on occasion one of the men has returned and has witnessed these anomalies of animals. I have to respect their privacy and will not disclose any information that will bring thrill seekers into the area.

More Bigfoot accounts:

In November of 1974 near Pigeon Mountain, the story recount: I was deer hunting on Pigeon Mountain and was following a group of deer when I shot and wounded an almost solid black buck with a large rack. The buck followed a well worn game trail and I had railed the deer by blood drops. It was getting dark and the terrain was getting to difficult to continue and I had no light. I had to turn and come down the mountain. I began to feel like I was not alone; there were none of the normal animal sounds. I heard something coming down the mountain taking a parallel path I was taking. I could not see anything. There were limbs breaking, leaves rustling and then I would hear nothing. I had unloaded my gun for safety and reloaded because I had never heard an animal move through the woods like this one.

Myself, one other person and the owner were the only people allowed to hunt in the area and the terrain it was using was too rough for a human to travel much less move at the speed this animal was. One minute is would sound like a raging bull and the next minute it would move down the mountain not making a sound. I heard a grunt and a growl. I was terrified and felt as I was being stalked by something I had never encountered before. When I stopped so did it. When I moved slowly, it moved slowly. When I moved faster, it moved faster. I was most worried when I would hear nothing.

I reached the base of the mountain and had taken a wrong turn and put myself in front of a large briar patch. I did not let that stop me. I dove through the briars cutting and scratching myself. I finally reached the safety of m truck and once again heard the grunting noise from behind me.

I did not return to look for the buck I had shot or ever hunt in that area again. I did not ever see anything, but something large was in the woods that night. I have not felt safe in the woods since. I had hunted, fished and farmed in the area all my life. I felt as though I knew all the animals in the woods and the sound they made as they moved. I was taught to stalk hunt by an employee who worked on our farm and he had lived in the Smokey Mountains and fed his family by hunting game. I had heard deer grunt before and this was no deer grunt.

The above anonymous person had more stories to tell about other locals personal experiences.

There had been stories of a creature that walked on two legs during that time period. There was an old dump on Shinbone Ridge where people would dump house garbage, rotten food and even dead animals. There were reported sighting there.

One farmer claimed to have chased such an animal in his pick-up in his field and could not catch it, running he said at 40 MPH. There were reports of large hogs being carried over tall fences with blood everywhere, missing dogs, missing livestock and strange noise..

One farmer said he saw a creature chasing his cows saying it was black had hair all over its body, moved on two legs but moved like a cat.

There was a rumor that an animal attacked a woman in a small car and nearly turned it over. The story I heard she claimed it was a deformed bear. Some people guessed the animal was a bear burned and scarred in fire or a genetically deformed bear that people were seeing..

My friends and I were camping and fishing at the foot of Pigeon and one of my friend brothers showed up at 2 AM and told us he heard an animal screaming behind his house not far away. He made us go back to his house. None of us heard anything.

In 1999 in a remote part of Pigeon a friend shot a deer, he dressed and hung it in a tree so it would not be gotten by a fox or coyote. He returned the next day, on his four wheeler, only to find the deer and his cleaning gear gone too without a trace.

I ran up and down the ridges to stay in shape during that time period, but I never saw the creature or any tracks. I heard noises I could not explain.

January 16, 1983- Another recount: Two friends of mine and me were pushing a cave lead in Cornfield Sink on the east side of Pigeon Mountain. We came out of the lead at about 3 AM and started gathering our caving gear together for the ½ mile walk to the car.

As we are about to leave the strangest call I have ever heard came from the opposite side of the sink from us. Distance would have been about 900 feet. The three of us have been woodsmen all our lives but none of us had ever heard a call like that. It sounded like four different animals in one. All powered by what must have been an enormous set of lungs. Hearing the vocalization the three of us looked at each other saucer eyed not saying a word. Each of us was hoping the other would pipe up with a logical explanation for what we had heard. Needless to say since we had been planning to leave anyway we beat a hasty retreat to the vehicles.

August 4, 1998 – Recount: My girlfriend and I traveled to this area at 11:30- that night to build a campfire and relax from the daily grind. She and I didn't have to work Wednesday, so the late hour didn't matter.

At about 11:30 we found a suitable site, approximately 7-8 miles in. There are only a dozen or so clearings for camping on the trail. Our site was on the trail, a clearing big enough to circle my truck around. It had two other trails at the back corners.

One didn't go far before the growth took over. The other looked like it might be passable, as far as I could tell. At 1 AM I was sitting on the tailgate and my girlfriend a few feet away tending the fire. Then we heard a loud high-pitched scream that reverberated through the dense forest. My girlfriend got scared and asked me what it was.

I have been an outdoorsman my whole life, hunting, fishing, camping and studying animals like a religion. I've never heard anything like that scream. I told my girlfriend to be quiet, maybe it would go off again.

The moon was high and bright to be not full yet. The trail was lit well, so I looked down the trail and I looked the way we came. In the middle of the trail a large, bulky figure stood! The way the light fell on its features I believe it was facing me from about 30 years distant. I thought at first it might be a tree or bush, but it had a discernable head, arms, torso, and legs.

I went and got my girlfriend, not saying anything to upset her. If it turned out to be a tree, she would be mad for me teasing her. I looked and the figure was gone! Back at the fire the "animal" behind us screamed same as before, except this time it sounded just inside the forest cover. Before we could react a similar, more distant call came from the forest in front of us.

Was this the thing I had seen? I don't know. At that I threw everything in the truck at my girlfriends panic. I shoveled sand on the fire while she screamed hurry! I jumped into that truck and hit out a lot fast than we drove in!

There are carnivorous plants within the boundaries of the park. These plants can be observed and shown to anyone by park employees.

There are snake stories of snakes so large that when laid in the back of pick up trucks they will hang off the tailgate. (I will not hike after dark there. In fact, that is a rule!)

Desperate pleas and screams in the night from what some people say are the uncrossed spirits of those who have taken their own lives in Little River Canyon or those who have met their death at the hands of a criminal.

UFO sightings have been reported as early as 1966.

I find that Little River Canyon is one of the most beautiful locations on this earth. As with anywhere that we don't obey the rules, listen carefully to those in charge we can have bad things happen to us. Fortunately for us, there are wonderful folks in charge there and you can enjoy the entire natural phenomenon along with an occasional paranormal experience.

Exquisite beauty is yours when you visit Little River Canyon!

The Mentone Springs Hotel

The Mentone Springs Hotel stands proudly on Lookout Mountain in Mentone, Alabama. The hotel has a very deep seeded history within the development of the Town of Mentone itself. To get where we are present owners Andy Talton and Mark Elacqua have brought back with resounding beauty what once the matriarch hotel of this lovely mountain top town. First we have to begin at the beginning.

Mentone

Mentone, "a singing stream," that trickles down
A mountainside, and hides among dense beds
Of laurel blooms. The sandstone cliffs in brown
And gray, lift up milkwort's and fame flower's heads
To see the sun go down behind sublime
Capped Cumberlands. The summer troops of heat
Arrive at Lookout's base, but cannot climb
The Slopes by day or night, and so defeat
Comes not to mar the cool, refreshing breeze
That stirs the hearts of men as well as trees.

Author Unknown

John Mason was a member of the first dragoons of the United States Calvary. He was a natural risk taker who led a life filled with adventure. Even when he had to travel west to partake in Calvary control of Native American uprisings he went with vigor. The battles went well but John Mason ended up with an Honorable Discharge due to serious injury. John loved the west so he decided to purchase a farm in Iowa. John Mason made a good living on his farm but by the age of 50 his health was in disarray. John had beliefs that the environment one lived in could be a controlling factor in health care issues. He tried and tried to find the perfect place even though his health was getting worse. He was visiting some friends and they told him about a man named Leavitt who lived on Lookout Mountain in Alabama. Leavitt went on and on to John about people who drank from the springs on Lookout Mountain had their illness's cured.

So John decided it was time to go and see for himself. Hopefully this place Lookout Mountain was the answer to his prayers. When John Mason arrived on Lookout Mountain he boarded with Leavitt's family within a very few months time after drinking and bathing in the miracle waters of the Mentone Springs he was as healthy as he ever been.

Since his health returned so did his thoughts of Iowa and his farm. He couldn't seem to get the thought of the money he was losing by being on Lookout Mountain which he didn't fathom he couldn't fathom he couldn't make a living here. So health be dammed he headed back to Iowa. Well no sooner than he got home to Iowa his health began to decline again. So he headed right straight back for Lookout Mountain.

In 1872 Mason returned to Iowa and gathered up the family. They all boarded a steamboat on the Mississippi River after they got as far as they could get by steamboat they traveled to Chattanooga by railroad. When they made it to Chattanooga the Mason family found that it was in the middle of a Cholera Epidemic. Therefore the Alabama Great Southern Trains weren't operating. John Mason had no choice but to buy a wagon and a team of horses to finish the journey to Lookout Mountain.

When the family arrived on the mountain they moved around a bit before they settled in. They lived at Lahusage for a time and Holly Springs which is south of Mentone and then finally he built a home directly up the mountain from Valley Head because it was closest to the post office. John also while not permanently settled in bought a piece of land we now call Moon Lake. John had a son named Ed in fact Ed is the one who named Moon Lake who went away to college and while there his thoughts swayed back to Lookout Mountain so intensely that he literally designed a town in his mind.

Ed was so happy as he put his thoughts to paper that he projected to everyone how exquisite, filled with nature, how remarkable the water was. His enthusiasm brought people to the mountain. One of those people was a Caldwell.

DR. JOHN LOGAN CALDWELL, one of the oldest practicing physicians of Rayland, Ohio has practically been a life-long resident of Jefferson County. He was born May 6, 1855 on the old farm in Mt. Pleasant Ridge, Warren Township, and Jefferson County, Ohio and is a son of Dr. John and Sarah E. (Patterson) Caldwell.

Dr. John Caldwell was born and reared in County Down, Ireland and after a common school education graduated from the Royal Infirmary at Glasgow, Scotland. He came to the United States about 1835 and located in Jefferson County, Ohio at Warrenton which was then a thriving little shipping point on the Ohio River. Here he embarked in the practice of his profession and about 1838 was united in marriage with Sarah R. Patterson, who was a daughter of Robert Patterson, one of the most prominent early settlers of this locality. Her father was the owner of several grist mills, had considerable bank stock, was also a large land owner and was extensively engaged in shipping on the river. Shortly after their marriage Dr. Caldwell located on one of the Patterson tracts on Mt. Pleasant Ridge and there engaged in the practice of medicine until the time of his death, March 17, 1868, when he was aged 58 years. Mrs. Caldwell died at Rayland, Ohio September, 1907 at the advanced age of 88 years. Dr. and Mrs. Caldwell were the parents of the following children: Jane, who is the widow of William Pickens; Sarah, widow of William McGruder; Robert; Maria, who is the wife of George Brown; James, deceased; John Logan, the subject of this record; Ella, who is the wife of Addison Burris; and Margaret, who married Thomas Shively.

John L. Caldwell was reared on the home farm, attended the district schools, Mt. Pleasant High School and Scio College, and at the age of eighteen began reading medicine with Dr. James G. Kennedy of New Market, now known as Scio, Ohio. Two years later he entered the Cleveland Medical College and in 1874 graduated from the College of Medicine and Surgery of Cincinnati, Ohio. August 18, of that same year he began the practice of medicine at Independence, Pa. and in 1875 located at West Middletown, Pa. where he remained one year in practice. He next practiced a short time at Wyandot City, Kansas and in March 1877, came to Rayland, then Portland Station, Ohio, where he has since successfully followed his profession.

Dr. Caldwell was married in August, 1876 to Elizabeth Wilson, of West Middletown, Pa. and to them was born two children: Mary, who married Cecil Collins, and has two children, Mary and Elizabeth; Sarah, who is the wife of Rev. C. F. Campbell and the mother of one daughter, Imogene. Mrs. Caldwell died in 1884 and in November, 1885, Dr. Caldwell married Anna Reddy, a native of Ireland, and of this union was born two children, **Alice** and **John** R. The latter will graduate with the class of 1912 from Starling Medical

College of Columbus, Ohio. Dr. Caldwell is politically identified with the Democratic party, and is fraternally affiliated with the F. and A. M., No. 182 of Smithfield. I found it quite nice that he named his daughter of his second marriage after he'd been with the family Mason in Mentone, Alice. Well after all Alice did come up with the name Mentone it is said.

Many people called J. L. (Frank). He was comfortable with that I suppose.

Sometime during 1884 the doctor boarded with the family of John Mason and built the Mineral Springs hotel. It is said the hotel was not finished until 1887. The style of the hotel is that of Queen Anne of the Victorian period with seven gables turrets dormer windows and veranda's. Dr. Caldwell oversaw everything but returned to Ohio in 1890 permanently. This writer believes that amongst all of the personal tragedy that Dr. Caldwell experienced in 1884 is exactly what brought him to Lookout Mountain.

Charles Loring of New Orleans, LA purchased the Mentone Springs Hotel around 1890. He changed the name to the Loring Springs Hotel. Charles worked hard to raise the hotel's stature among travelers until it competed well with the famous Lookout Mountain Hotel's in Chattanooga, TN.

In or about 1914 the hotel was sold to A.A. Chapman and Dr. J. N. Chaney of Rome, GA. They are the ones who built what is now called The White Elephant, a two story annex that contained 24 rooms with private baths. The water for the baths was pumped all the way from Little River. The peak season for the hotel was from June 1 to October 1. Today with the camps you could say the dates are about the same. The new owners advertised swimming, fishing, tennis, bowling, croquet, billiards, box golf, dancing, and a playground for children. They also advertised heavily both springs on the property: Mineral Springs and Beauty Springs for their curative powers. Beauty Springs was a short walk of 200 yards along a shaded pathway. Mineral Springs on the other hand had a two story pavilion sheltering it.

One guest of the hotel, a Dr. John E. Purdon who had been a British Army Surgeon tried to start an English Colony at Mentone. Needless to say he failed. But there is much more about Dr. Purdon in reference to the beginning history of the Camp Laney location. It began in 1887 when Dr. John Edward Purdon and his wife Katherine came from Athlone, Ireland, with their servants to Mentone.

In Mentone he was a practicing physician and did so much of the time without monetary payment giving much to the community. There is only a portion of remains of the old fireplace that stands where the Purdon family lived on Camp Laney. The Purdon's are buried at Bankhead Cemetery.

In 1918 John B. and Bert A. Ingram who were brothers from Birmingham, AL purchased the property. They were the organizers of the Mentone Hotel and Realty Company. The brothers had no desire to run the hotel so they hired Frank A. Robertson who was a professional hotel operator as the manager and had their sister Jessica served as hostess. Jessica only did this during the second season.

In 1920 the Alabama Baptist State Convention wanted to purchase the hotel along with 200 Acres of land for summer camp. They found out real quick that the Baptist State Convention couldn't do it. So to go around this and acquire the property eight Baptist formed a private Corporation to make the purchase. They provided that the Baptist convention would have assembly privileges for 10 years.

The first convention was attended 110 young people of the Baptist Young People Union in August 1921. A decision was made to hold the conventions in June of each year and the remainder of the year the accommodations were offered to the general public. The last convention was held in 1931. Even with 8 owners not one of them was able to maintain the hotel because of the Great Depression. The group leased the hotel to many operators but none could seem to bring the hotel back. One of the leasers was "Hello" F. L. Ferrell and his wife Nina. Therefore they decided to close it.

One of the group, Ed H. Moore of Birmingham bought out the stock from the other 7 and sold it to the J. L. Todd Company of Rome, GA.

As unfortunate as this may sound the masses came together as on July 4, 1950 all the buildings and lots were sold at auction to the highest bidders. Mr. Ben Hammond chooses to buy the hotel for use of a family summer home. H. L.

Murphy of Summerville, GA bought the annex. The annex then became the Sunset Hotel. Mr. Murphy sold the Sunset Hotel to Frank Young and Frank Rotch and the hotel became known as the "White Elephant."

Norville Hall purchased the hotel property around 1954. As you will see below Mr. Hall received his education in music from the American Conservatory of Music in Chicago. Mr. Hall played wind instruments (the pipe organ and more) professionally in both his home town of Birmingham, Alabama as well as Chicago, Illinois. Norville had a pipe organ shipped by train from Ohio to Mentone in pieces. It was hauled up the mountain and he literally put part of it in the attic and part in the basement as well as the main part in the downstairs of the hotel. Norville used the hotel as a storage facility for many organ and musical instruments parts to repair any instruments in need that were sent to him.

Norville Hall seeks piano pupils

Parents who are interested in providing a musical background for their children will be happy to learn that Norville Hall of Chicago, is accepting piano pupils in Palatine on Saturday mornings. Mr. Hall received his musical education at the American Conservatory of Music in Chicago. He has been a successful teacher of piano, organ, and theory in Chicago and has played professionally in Chicago and Birmingham, Ala.

For information or appointment, phone Mercia Heise, Palatine 102-M. Call at 333 W. Slade St.

This was taken from the Daily Herald (Chicago, Illinois) The Palentine Press September 5, 1941

During Mr. Hall's ownership of the Mentone Springs Hotel he sold all the wood off the side of the building. The wood was used by locals to erect their houses.

Photo Courtesy of Andy Talton

Needless to say the hotel was in total disrepair for some time. Norville Hall died while on stage in Salem, Massachusetts in 1979. His mother and sister retained ownership until later in the year then it was sold by the Hall estate to Ray and Sandra Padgett.

In September 1980 the hotel was purchased by Ray and Sandra Padgett of Atlanta, GA. Ray and Sandra put all their energies into restoration as well. Structurally the hotel was a mess so they immediately had the building jacked up and leveled. The building was literally collapsed on either end! The Padgett's put their hearts into the Hotel and in the end had to sell the hotel and did so to Charlie Johnson. It is important to note that during the Padgett's ownership the hotel received listing with The Alabama Historical Register on October 20, 1983 it was added to the National Register of Historic Places by the U.S. Department of Interior.

Charlie Johnson spent a considerable amount of money trying to turn the hotel back around again. Mr. Johnson had to replace all the missing exterior wood but still had serious problems with the interior.

Photo Courtesy of Andy Talton

He had to close off all the guest rooms due to the fact that the building had sank from extreme roof leaking and water weight as well as ground shifting and settling. Charlie attacked the main room (front room), dining room and parlor room.

Charlie added a full industrial kitchen and opened a lovely

restaurant. The Mentone Springs hotel was finally partially in its restoration phase. The money Charlie had spent was overwhelming in such a short period of time so he sold within a year to the Wassom's.

Claudia and Dave Wassom purchased the Mentone Springs hotel and moved from Northern California to renovate and run the Nineteenth Century Inn. Claudia left the Silicon Valley management job with Bechtel Group Inc. to run the hotel. David, her husband gave up his 26 (twenty-six) year dental practice to become its chef. The Wassom's set up the Mentone Springs hotel to be an artist commune. The initial idea was to have the artist in one room and in the connecting room their art. The Wassom's attempted to follow through with their dream for the hotel but it didn't survive.

Photo Courtesy of Andy Talton

Then we come to the Mentone Springs Hotel's final salvation!

Do you believe in 'signs' from a higher being? Well this author does so when you read this little story of how Andy Talton and Marc Elacqua became the owners of The Mentone Springs Hotel you just might too.

Andy Talton whose expertise is in the line of Marketing & Design was contracted by the owners of the Lodge of Gorham Bluff in Pisgah, Alabama. This job was no small feat. Andy, as expected did a wonderful job and wanted to share the joy of completion with his life partner Marc. On September 10, 2001, the fellows headed from Atlanta where they both resided with dogs in tow to Pisgah for Marc to have a first hand look at Andy's work.

While driving along Highway 117, Andy was admiring the small town of Mentone and noticed a FOR SALE sign at the Mentone Springs Hotel and asked Marc to stop. Marc did not give in, he drove on discouraging Andy due to the fact that they had a lovely old farmhouse in North Carolina that they had been working at every opportunity they could get off work to go. They had no such thing as a vacation there it was going to repair and upgrade. You see Marc knew Andy so well he already knew what was about to happen.

There was no disappointment in the Gorham Lodge project. Andy's work was a success! Then it was time for a return ride back to Atlanta. Same route as you can suspect. Andy could not get the Mentone Springs Hotel off his mind and pleaded with Marc to stop! As you can surmise Marc gave in and indeed stopped. Oh my, a mess to behold. When they graced the doors of the hotel, it was in shambles. From holes in the floors to moth balls in the urinals, this was such a mess. As you can imagine there was a battle to be waged here. Andy and Marc continued on to Atlanta with thoughts of how something so beautiful had come to such a disaster. Both of them knew the hotel had potential but whether or not they were willing to do it the answer would come later.

The next day was a day in history we will all never forget. The Twin Towers had tumbled down with ferocity from the terrorist attacks of September 11, 2001. The impact of all those lives lost was so traumatic. God Bless all those families today and forever.

The impact spread wide and far. The economy took a hit as many businesses both large and small were closed. Both Andy and Marc were affected as well. Their jobs became non-existent due to the economic impact. So for them their lives as they knew it had changed significantly and would start a new very soon. They both owned homes in the Atlanta area. They made a choice. Mentone it was! They put both their homes on the market and purchased the Mentone Springs Hotel on November 1, 2001.

They hit the Mentone Springs hotel with a vengeance. They began with interior improvements, patching up all the holes so that they could keep vermin and reptiles out. All the plumbing and electrical had to be completely redone. They transported much of their furnishings from their North Carolina farm as well as their furnishing from their Atlanta homes to Mentone. They were forced to burn some of the furnishings that had been left by the Wassom family due to exposure.

Andy and Marc created a schedule on how to bring the rooms up for use. They would start of Thursday by dismantling it then on Friday and Saturday bringing the room up to speed and redecorating and Sunday putting the finishing touches to it. They did this until they had ten rooms complete, making some into suites.

In 2002, Andy and Marc opened "Caldwell's Restaurant" bringing back the birth of fine dining to the hotel. You can sit inside an exquisitely decorated restaurant or be seated on the veranda while you eat and enjoy the fresh air and beauty of Mentone.

Now what would a little history be without tales of haunting? It is said that on a full moon one can sit on the Mentone Square and see a beautiful lady in a flowing white gown slowly moving across the second floor veranda. I think I might sit one night and see.

Mentone Springs Hotel circa 1970
Photo Credit Unknown

Photo credit unknown

Until I have that opportunity let me share with you one of four eye witness accounts this author was able to acquire during the research phase of The Mentone Springs Hotel. There we so many residents of the Hotel over the years, so many stories told….so many things that were not explainable from behaviors to activity. This particular ghostly entity I penned the white lady since in the beginning I thought I was the only one who had seen her. But no! That was not the case at all!

From those still living I found a lady who lives in Chattanooga, who along with her mother lived at the Mentone Springs Hotel during the "Padgett" era. The mother Ms. Lucy Mitchell was a lovely lady and quite the artist indeed. Today you will find her art gracing the walls at the Mentone Springs Hotel.

Lucy's daughter who said that growing up at the Hotel was "certainly different" but "nice" had an experience oh so many years ago that she had kept close, only sharing with family and the best of friends.

While lying asleep in her first floor bedroom around 3 AM, Nancy was stirred by the sound of a kitten. Off the covers came, as she headed out the door to go in search of the lost furry one. Nancy always loved animals so getting up and taking off was not out of the ordinary for her. Nancy headed out turned towards the post office and continued to walk as she continued to hear the meow's of the kitten. All the way and no sign of a kitten yet! How frustrated she was! She turned and began walking back to the Hotel. In the distance she sees "**something**", in front of the Hotel next to the road. As Nancy gets closer the image gets clearer. It's a lady, dressed in a white dress with a hoop skirt and she's drawing water from a well.

Nancy tried to shake off what she was seeing. **Number 1**, there was NO well in front of the Hotel. **Number 2**, she hadn't heard of any local masquerade parties.

Nancy stopped and stared at the lady so intensely that the lady in the white dress turned to face Nancy. The lady had the bluest eyes and was wearing some type of coverlet over her hair.

Then they are both shocked that they are staring at each other and "*Poof*"…there goes the Lady in the White Dress. Nancy decides not to go in the front door; she scoots around to the back and heads in the back door.

This same apparition has been validated by three other folks therefore I far as I can tell since the people are not close nor knew each others stories makes the entity validated for me.

The Mentone Inn

In 1954 the Mentone Inn was called the DeSoto Lodge

Today's memories of the Mentone Inn began with the dream of one man of having a boarding house for those who were in the community as workers without family homes, for wayward travelers to have a place to lay their heads when weary from travel and for those who'd come upon hard times and could no longer afford a home to call their own. H.B. Gillette erected a two story boarding house in 1873 along the brow of LookOut Mountain in the heart of Mentone, Alabama.

As you've read through this book you are aware that the town of Mentone has not been named yet. In the yard of this boarding house to the slight west direction was a "General Store". To those who lived in this era, a general store carried everything from feed to seed, cloth to shoes, and medicine to your mail. John Mason had erected this store on his own property of course as John owned most all of what is current day Mentone.

John made his son Ed Mason the very first postmaster of this area. Ed was the postmaster from March 10, 1888 until April 27, 1891. Delivery of mail began on horseback from town to town and then evolved to horse and buggy from Valley Head.

The store continues in the Mentone Inn family as James Huron and his family moved to Mentone on February 8, 1899 from Ohio. It took the Huron's less than a year to purchase the store and the two-story house from H.B. Gillette on April 1, 1900.

Then unexpectedly the Huron's sold the property back to H.B. Gillette! But there was a certain stipulation: Mrs.

Huron, Mentone's first Post Mistress who had became such on October 12, 1899, was not to have completed her term until June 19, 1900 so she was to be allowed this time.

H.B. Gillette took possession of the property on May 1, 1900. On July 15th, 1900, the Huron family loaded up and headed to Indianapolis, Indiana. During the next year Mr. Gillette again sold the property, this time to a Mr. P. K. Smith.

Even though the Huron's were in Indianapolis, a part of their hearts was still on this lovely mountain. They communicated with Mr. Smith, the new owner and returned to Mentone on February 18, 1903, not only as residents but as the owners of the store property and the boarding house. The store needed some repairs so it was a month before they could reopen it and then in August they took possession of the boarding house.

Makes a person wonder just what went on with the Huron's and the Gillette's.

Mrs. Huron operated the boarding house until she died in July of 1920. Mrs. Huron was intense about the boarding house. It is said her presence can be felt at times.

Photo Courtesy of "Landmark" circa 1890

Halbert (Olie) Howe was born February 29, 1884 in Talmadge, Ohio. Hal came to Alabama in 1907 where he worked as the Post Master in Lahusage for the mines.

He also worked in the commissary with Fred Huron. It was here that he met Elizabeth Lizzie Green, the daughter of Stephen Green and Achsah Olivea Culberson. The two were married in 1908.

Hal Howe rented the Mentone Inn property in 1922 with an option to purchase the land at a later date. He converted the store to a kitchen and used the dining room as a new business called "Hal's House". This business did well for the next five years. Progress was in the making. Highway 117 was being built; the mountainside path being blasting was the cause of many problems though for Mentonians.

The blasts as we know crumpled the outlet for the historic Mineral Springs but Hal Howe did not know that it had loosened the mortar so seriously in his fireplace that when the fire was lit the first time in winter of 1927 the place went up in smoke. It took Hal less than a year to have it back up and running. His determination speaks volumes.

Photo Courtesy of Harriet Pentz (Private Collection)

Photo's Courtesy of Harriet Pentz (Private Collection)

Hal Howe was known as a man who offered so much to his guests at the Hal's Hotel. He would take them as far as Chattanooga for entertainment. Many guests returned time after time. Hal later changed the name of his hotel to the DeSoto Hotel. We believe this to have been during the time following the death of his first wife Elizabeth in July 1929. Three and a half months following her death on November 10, 1929, he remarried to Nelda Estelle Ellis.

The Ellis family of which this author has familial connection settled in DeKalb County in the very early 1800's. Hal wrote a book in 1930 called "Mentone & My Philosophy".

In September of 1954 Hal sold the DeSoto Hotel to H. H. Plotts of Coral Gables, Florida, near Miami. The Plotts immediately changed the name of the Hotel to the DeSoto

Lodge. For the next 23 years, until 1977, the Plotts called the DeSoto Lodge their home.

A native of Mentone, Amelia Kirk Brooks who was married to Robert Brooks of California bought the hotel and brought it back to Mentonian family ownership in 1977.

Amelia could not wait to change the name from DeSoto Lodge to The Mentone Inn. The name we all know and love. As Amelia has told many, "It didn't look like a lodge, it looked like and Inn, so it was!"

Amelia being torn from family here in Mentone, the Inn and family in California began trying to find the perfect ones to operate the Inn. She sold the Inn to Mr. & Mrs. Nesbitt in 1979. They changed the name of the Inn to Mountain View Inn. The Nesbitts had a few problems and Amelia ended back up with the Inn. And as you can guess it went back to the Mentone Inn.

Still being torn with being across the country, Amelia leased the Inn to Mr. Ray Cox of Gadsden, Alabama. During this time there are stories upon stories of private rooms, etc. Drop by the Inn sometime and ask the Innkeeper Gloria to fill you in. So many indeed that Amelia ended back up with the Inn again.

Amelia found another couple of folks, literally two couples: Mr. & Mrs. Bill McCarty and Mr. & Mrs. Glenn Franklin. Their stay as Innkeepers was short lived as they returned the Inn to Amelia.

Finally Amelia found someone to buy the Inn by the names

of Frances and Karl Waller in 1995. It is said that Mrs. Waller spent a tremendous amount of money filling the Inn with antiques and upgrades.

Much later the Inn came up for Auction and was purchased by the Mike Campbell's of Birmingham, Alabama. It is my pleasure to share the "meant to be" story of the auction. By an act of fate a friend of Mike Campbell's was an auctioneer and was about to have an auction of the Mentone Inn property in Mentone, Alabama.

Mike and Sarah Campbell had always enjoyed the Mentone area but the flyer of the auction seemed to find its way to the bottom of the desk.

On the day of the auction was also the day of the Red/White game in Tuscaloosa of the Crimson Tide that Mike Campbell was planning to attend. In fact he got up that day in 1999 and prepared to go. Sarah Campbell had other ideas. Sarah was thinking about how nice it would be to have a family retreat in Mentone. So Sarah said to Mike, "Why don't we go to the Auction at Mentone of the Inn?" Mike had actually all be forgotten the event.

To appease Sarah and because something was kind of knawing at his inner peace Mike agreed to go. Change of plans!!

Sarah said to Mike as they were driving down the road that they would have to have a certified check for $10000.00 to even participate in the Auction. Mike looked at Sarah and asked her in all seriousness if she planned on participating.

From the smile on Sarah's face he thought, that's a yes! So here go Mike and Sarah to their bank, actually in a rush as it was closing at noon to get a check from savings for the $10,000 needed to bid.

Upon arrival in Mentone Mike says it was like someone began showing them around like they were the only ones there, but of course they weren't.

The bidding begins! Sarah is in the heat of the bid back and forth she goes feverishly with a young brunette from Georgia. The thousand increments had finally made it down to 1,000. And the bid was up to 285,000.00 Sarah had won!!!!

Mike said it took the two of them three days or so to figure out what they'd won and just how much money it was going to cost. He smiles now in retrospect. The Inn was meant to be theirs.

They drove back up to the Inn to take possession and without a semblance of time passing the phone begins to ring with clients wanting to secure their reservations which some had been making for forty years or more. Each year the same families had traditions and some of those had the tradition of staying at the Mentone Inn. Mike and Sarah's plan of family retreat was not going to work. Mike and Sarah had bought a business and now had to figure out how to become Innkeepers.

There only choice was to hire an Innkeeper and they did so and then another and another until the lovely Miss Gloria came along.

For the last three years the Mentone Inn has been home to the famous "Memphis Annie", Ms. Gloria Sitz who rents the Inn from the Campbell's' and is fulfilling her dream as an Innkeeper and bringing the "Blues" back to Mentone with her T. A. G. Blues Society and the many festivals she brings to Mentone.

Oh this story has so many ways it can go on the haunting but I'll share just a few hints as to where one can have the possibility of a haunting experience.

In Cherokee Room, a male spirit who seems to be stuck and just can't cross over seems to weave in and out of time there.

Many people have heard footsteps when there is simply no one about.

A ball can be left inside a glove in one room only to come back later and see the ball is out and rolling around the room.

Many magical and spiritual experiences have been shared by many at the Mentone Inn. And as you can guess I think that my relative, Nelda Ellis Howe has something to do with that ;).

And of course there is the mysterious boarder. On more than one occasion a gentlemen dressed in suit, overcoat and dress hat has knocked on the door of the Inn late at night needing accommodations. He is always shown to a room. The following morning there is no notice that the man was even present at the Inn. Nothing!

Please remember to visit the Mentone Inn while in the area.

Photo Courtesy of Darren Vallence

Mentone, a place the Great God built,
Up near the sunlit sky.
Where life is new and friends are true
And days too quickly fly;
Where wearied souls regain their power
And sorrows leave in the night
Where peace is born with each new morn
A haven of joy and delight.

Written by Sidney Lanier Gibson
Gifted to Mr. and Mrs. W.E. Hargrove
Former operators of the Mentone Hotel

The Hitching Post

The "Hitching Post" Circa 1951

The **"Hitching Post"** known by many for so many years became the "Crow's Nest" after being purchased by the Crow Family. Today you see an antique store, the Gourdie Shop and a small real estate office in this once infamous complex. The sounds that permeated from the upstairs as couples danced the night away. Men drank booze during the great depression and talked of fast times and how they would make their "nitch" in society. Later the upstairs became a dance hall for square dancing and for youth across the county to come and enjoy fabulous times! Downstairs there was a store where fuel could be purchased or a few groceries.

The Mentone Store was actually built by Guy Burgess in 1898. His first move was to bring the Post Office from the Gillette Store located at the site of the current Mentone Square. Mr. Burgess was the Post Master from September 9, 1902 for the next five years until September 10, 1907.

Mr. Burgess sold the store to Mr. D. L. Jones and then Mr. Jones sold it to Lowe & Pierce who actually operated the store for several years. Mr. Sam Graham held the mortgage for the store and when Lowe & Pierce met with financial problems Mr. Graham took the mortgage back upon default of payments.

Mr. Sam Graham decided to build the dance hall. Rather than rip the roof off the building he simply had the contractor lift the floor and bracing four feet up, so there is still a roof under the dance hall floor!

The dance hall was one of few in the area and brought great joy and fellowship to the surrounding area. This author finds that plenty of alcohol was available during the times of prohibition and was enjoyed by those dancing if they so chose through stories of those with proper knowledge.

Another note Homer Crow told me that when he was a small boy that upon entering the "Hitching Post" through the double doors on the right side there were three slot machines. I figured those game machines. Homer showed me with the arm motion of pulling down that they were indeed slot machines of some type.

On the east end of the building where the Gourdie Shop now is you would have found the Post Office. Neighbors would gather together in the afternoons and await the arrival of news from friends and family across the country.

When Mr. Sam Graham passed away he left the property to Eleanor Graham Glover and John Graham who in turn deeded it to Alexander Glover. Alexander then sold the property to Mr. and Mrs. Fritz Smith.

Doc and Kyle Long bought the property from the Smiths and they in turn sold it to Bernice and Homer Crow; in 1979. Following Bernice's death the property now belongs to their lovely daughter, Doreen, who sells antiques in a majority of the property.

The Hitching Post has a wonderful history as you can tell it was a general store, gas station, a restaurant and the meeting place for the fox hunters before going on the hunt.

As far as the Haunting of this location goes: Story has it that a lady has been heard crying upstairs, seen wandering up and down the dance floor from the outside on moonlit nights. I wonder if she's just locked in time, a residual energy. Sounds like it to me.

Graham Manor

While walking down a side street in Mentone we came upon a home that takes you back into time, at least in my mind it did. On the grounds you find a boxwood maze just like those found on the grounds of castles in Europe. I walked through the maze and felt as though I had become Alice in Wonderland seeking an end to the trail. A variation of aroma's permeated my nose as fragrances from the garden seep through.

After escaping the maze I head back out the wrought iron gate that has aged with time as is seen with a slight rust coating. A massive home stands before me as I am drawn to it looking up into a dormer window and it appears a lady is looking back at me inviting me with her eyes to enter into her world.

This home called "Graham Manor" was built by John Graham for his mother Ms. "Teeney" Eleanor Glover. The original structure was a "fishing cabin" for his Uncle Samuel Glover.

Mr. John Graham was the third curator for the Williamsburg, Virginia Museum. John was a serious collector of 19th century Folk Art. John Graham worked side by side with Jackie Kennedy in the White House when she became the

First Lady and had the ominous job of redoing the White House as all First Lady's face. The style of Jackie was aided by John during this era. John Graham molded his selections of furnishings into the White House for all to see. If the furnishing did not fit the White House it would definitely fit Graham Manor and it found a home there.

Mr. John Graham was quite a fascinating man. In his honor on the mantle of Graham Manor is this portrait as well as a story from the Birmingham Museum that gives you an idea of just how generous a man he was. I hope you enjoy reading it.

John Graham

Mr. Graham, a native of Georgia, was for many years on the curatorial staff of the Brooklyn Museum and afterwards, was for seventeen years Director of Collections for Colonial Williamsburg.

Mr. Graham retired to Northern Alabama in the early 1970-'s. Over the years Mr. Graham assembled an extraordinary collection of paintings and decorative arts. The loan of these objects enable the museum to fill important and necessary gaps in its growing collection of "American nineteenth-century paintings, and to exhibit American and English furniture of this caliber.

The ceramics, especially the earthenware, will enhance the museum's collection presently strong in eighteenth century Wedgwood and English and Continental porcelain. Mr. Graham's collection includes some twenty-seven paintings by both well-known and Native American artists. Among the eighteenth-century works is a most inhering and problematic painting of a young girl with an American parrot; whether the painting itself is American or Dutch remains to be determined.

From the late century is a fine portrait by John Wollaston and a second by Joseph Badger. A group of exceptionally fine nineteenth-century landscape paintings is dominated by the Wind River Valley, Wyoming by Albert Bierstadt, which in turn is accompanied by two of Bierstadt's studies of the Villa D'Este, completed on his first trip to Rome, Bierstadt's study of cloud formations, and studies of animals made while Bierstadt was on an early trip to the American West.

Other nineteenth-century paintings include works by Asher B. Durand, John F. Kensett, Thomas Chambers, Frances Clark, Robert Loftin Newman and W. A. Miller, John F. Peto and Leon Moran. Included in the decorative arts are twenty six examples of American and English furniture, dating from the late seventeenth century to the early nineteenth century.

From Rhode Island is a pair of mahogany side chairs with a vase-shaped splat and arch crest rail dating from the late eighteenth century, and a tiger-grained maple desk with a slanting lid and bracket feet dating to the third quarter of the eighteenth century.

From Pennsylvania are several handsome examples of furniture including a walnut side chair with a vase splat, delicately curved crest rail and trepid feet. The chair retains its original leather seat and dates 1750 1760. Also from Pennsylvania are a walnut drop leaf dining table in the Chippendale style with cabriole legs and ball and claw fee, ca. 1750-60, a mahogany card table with reeded legs, ca 1800-1810, and a mahogany "birdcage" tripod table with snake feet and circular top, from Philadelphia, ca 1760-1780.

The exhibition includes additional examples from England, New York and New England as well as a few from the South. Objects from the latter include a tea table of southern mahogany which is attributed to Norfolk, Virginia, a Helpplewhite style sideboard with delicate inlay attributed to Savannah, Georgia, ca 1790-1810, and finally a cherry corner cupboard with a chamfered corners, scroll top and elaborate inlay in geometric and floral motifs. This piece is attributed to Morristown, Tennessee, first quarter of the nineteenth century.

The ceramics are highlighted by especially fine English eighteenth-century, tin glazed earthenware punch bowls and plates, two Whieldon-type plates and agateware teapot, five salt glaze plates, a finely enameled salt glaze teapot and elaborate three-tier, cream ware epergne.

Also included, besides other examples of English and Continental, are porcelains from England and the Continent.

The Museum Board and Staff are grateful to Mr. Graham for making his many objects available for a long term loan. These works will make a significant addition to the permanent collections, most of the objects in *which have been generously donated by many friends of the museum. The collection of nineteenth-century American paintings and furniture will be enhanced dramatically.*

"Birmingham Museum of Art"

Writer Unknown

The Camps of Mentone

The camps of Mentone are without a doubt has a huge economic impact on the town of Mentone and surrounding areas. Many provide year around income for quite a few employees. The camps are not restricted to just the Alabama side of LookOut Mountain but also extend over into the Georgia side.

Camp Alanita:

Camp Alanita was an exclusive girls camp that lay at the base of Eagle's Nest, a very unusual rock formation that leads one to definitely believe this area was under water at one time. The camp was built in 1923 by Nick Lowrey and his wife along with his cousin Russell Lowry and Nick Davenport of Valley Head. The Nick Lowrey's were from Nashville, Tennessee. This unusually located camp was operated for three years then moved up the road and ran for two more years, and then closed.

Camp DeSoto:

Camp DeSoto is known to be the oldest camp in Mentone. The camp is located on Little River just about a mile to the east of Mentone. The Camp has forty-eight buildings and consists of three separate camps within one large one. There are four two week sessions during the summer. The Camp has its own library located in the lodge. The gym has a stage that is multi-purpose and used as a stage, also for sports, parties and church services.

Mrs. Ada Newton of Illinois along with her nephew Curtis Springer opened Camp DeSoto as a boy's camp. The camp was not quite the success as had been hoped for. When Mrs. Newton passed away her attorney inherited the Boys camp. Her attorney, Mr. Aherns, in turn rented out the property to a Mr. Young and a Mr. Orr of Birmingham, Alabama. They ran the camp as both a girls and boys camp for seven years from 1928-1935. Miss Eloise Hart and Miss Bess Cook bought out the gentlemen from Birmingham and rented the property from Mr. Aherns from 1935-36. Nelda Howe stated in her book on Mentone that Miss Harts sister, Mrs. Davies, was the one who supervised the camp. Miss Hart bought out Miss Cook in 1937 and continued to operate the camp until 1945. Miss Hart sold a portion of the property to Miss Bess Heron, Mrs. Norma Bradshaw and Miss Sue Henry in 1945. Miss Herron and Mrs. Bradshaw retired in the mid 70's. Miss Sue Henry took over as the owner and then sold to Phil and Marsha Hurt. The Hurt's are the current owners.

Camp Cloudmont:

This camp was set up on 40 acres in 1924 by the Miami, Florida, YMCA. The camp was operated by C.W. Ables and L.B. Somers. In 1930 the two gentlemen purchased the camp along with a friend, Charles W. Edwards. There are over forty buildings today and was owned by Jack Jones for several years. This is a private camp for boys. Camp Cloudmont was changed to Riverview and is now owned by Susan and Larry Hooks.

Lookout Mountain Camp:

This is a camp for boys. This camp was opened in 1927 by Dr. J.A. Gorman and his son in law Gray D. Morrison of New Orleans. It is now owned by John Morrison the son of Gray D. Morrison and is a religious retreat and Boys Camp.

Skyline Camp:

This camp was established by Eloise Hart Temple as a girl's camp. Mrs. Temple had a girls senior house on the brow which has graffiti all over the second floor walls from the girls still to this day. The house is on the Sunset Rock property. After Mrs. Temple retired Miss Mary Griffin took over. The camp is now owned by Sally Johnson Cash.

Alpine Lodge:

This lodge was started by Milford Howard in 1926. He operated it until 1934 when a Miss Alice McVickers of Miami, Florida purchased the lodge and founded Alpine Lodge Camp for Girls which she operated until 1959. In 1959 Rufus Hyde of Dallas, Texas and Richard O'Ferrell, Jr. of Jackson, Mississippi bought it and established a boy's camp. Hyde retired in 1962 and O'Ferrell still continues on.

Camp Laney:

This camp was founded in 1959 by Coach Malcolm Laney who was the Assistant Coach at the University of Alabama and former head coach of Woodlawn High School in Birmingham, Alabama. The Coach and his wife Louise started the camp in 1959 and continued to operate it for fifteen years. This camp is located on Little River at the former location of Riverdale Lodge that burned in the 30's. It is now owned by the Mayor of Mentone, Rob Hammond formerly of Rome, GA who is an educator. Rob purchased Camp Laney in 1974. Rob graduated from Vanderbilt University. His wife San helps him run the camp. Camp Laney has some wonderful facilities as I had the opportunity to view first hand.

Camp Laney has a swimming pool, a riding ring, an athletic field and archery/rifle ranges. Camp Laney has excellent medical facilities for ill or injured campers.

Camp Laurel Dell:

This camp was built in 1956 by Dolores Morgadanes of New Orleans. The property is now owned by Alexander Glover of Rome, GA. The Glovers changed the name to Camp High River.

Camp Comer Scout Reservation:

The largest camp in the area has over 1,000 acres. The camp belongs to the eleven- county Choccolocco Council of the Boy Scouts of America. The camp was opened officially on June 8, 1965.

The land had been purchased in 1962 and the camp was named after Hugh Ross Comer of Sylacauga, Alabama, who had served as a long time scout worker and at that time was the president of the Choccolocco Council.

Within two years over 3,000 scouts and leaders had attended Camp Comer. On the property there is a ninety acre lake. The lake is named Lake Republic in honor of the former Republic Steel Plant in Attalla which was a major financial supporter of the Camp.

Camp Ponderosa Bible Camp:

Ponderosa Bible Camp consists of 80 acres along Little River just five miles north of Mentone. The Camp was founded in 1973 by the University of Alabama. Dr. Henry Rikard and Michael Dinoff who were professors of Psychology at the University established this camp for emotionally disturbed children and for those with learning disabilities.

The Camp has twelve buildings for their staff, a dining hall, a chapel and six cabins.

This camp is operated by the Children's Bible Mission of Lakeland, Florida. The local director is Glenn Miller.

Sherry Snyder Private Collection

Alpine Lodge

Sherry Snyder Private Collection

Mentone Springs Hotel

(Unknown Photo Credit)

White Elephant formerly The Sunset Hotel

Sherry Snyder Private Collection

The Eagles Nest

Sherry Snyder Private Collection

The Swinging Bridge at Alpine Lodge

Sherry Snyder Post Card Private Collection

Deborah Collard, RN

Author

Psychic Medium, Remote Viewer, Practicing Shaman, Paranormal Investigator

Deborah Collard, who is Cherokee by blood, enjoys reaching back into the past to connect her with the spiritual world. The way she celebrates this passion is through her studies of the paranormal.

Deborah considers herself an 'oldie' in this venue, knowing that 30 years ago the only tools she used to investigate with were her flashlight and whomever she could drag along with her to see if she could find answers to the many questions that wandered through her mind.

As technology progressed so did she and many years later has a very solid team of paranormal investigators. The Team is NAPS - Northeastern Alabama Paranormal Society based out of Guntersville, Alabama. NAPS was officially formed in 2003. Deborah teaches workshops, does lectures and panels on the paranormal. It is important to her that ghost hunters know just what they are doing and the proper way to do it.

Deborah has two previously published books to her credit. These books are "Haunted Southern Nights®" Vol. 1, Ghost Hunting the Basics and "Haunted Southern Nights®" Vol. 2, The Haunted Backyard and now "Haunted Southern Nights®, The History and Haunting of the Mentone Area."

Deborah continued her studies in the paranormal by completing post secondary education offered by the HCH Institute under the direction of Loyd Auerbach to receive a certification in Parapsychological Studies. For the past several years Deborah has trained many paranormal investigators and continues to lecture and panel in her region on the paranormal. She also assists law enforcement agencies, private investigators and families using her psychic abilities to help find closure of not only the cases but the 'not knowing' associated with them for the families. Deborah is an active member of the Parapsychological Association and of the United Cherokee Ani-Yun-Wiya Nation. Also she is a member of the Alabama State Board of Nursing as a Registered Nurse. Deborah is currently attending classes for her certification in Forensic Nursing.

Deborah is the host of NAPS Live Radio "Haunted Southern Nights®" which airs live each Tuesday night on Blogtalk Radio.

Psychic Abilities: Having psychic ability is sometimes a blessing, sometimes a curse. My psychic abilities consist of clairvoyance, clairsentience and clairaudience with familial precognition. I've helped many with all of these 'gifts'. Remote viewing is something that I've done to assist families with loved ones lost by violent crimes. I see through the eyes of the victim which granted is better than seeing through the eyes of the perpetrator. It is also something that I utilize as a psychic to help others see into. Also I can use remote viewing techniques to do as one would say "a psychic reading". My preparation for these events is much disciplined as I meditate and follow meticulous rituals to prepare my mind for the openness needed prior to delving into such a feat. Helping people through my psychic abilities has been my salvation. The Creator blesses us in many ways, some of us differently than others. I must put forth the effort to do the "right" thing with this blessed gift by sharing and teaching others. I hope to have many opportunities to do just that before my time on this earth has ended in this physical form.

Radio Shows: NAPS Live Radio, Darkness on the Edge of Town Radio, The Cari Stone Show, SOPR on Now Live, SNEP Radio, Doc J Radio and many more.

Newspaper: The Advertiser Gleam, The Times Journal (many times), The Magical Buffet, The Sand Mountain Reporter, The Daily Sentinel, The Chattanooga News Free Press, The Birmingham News, The LookOut View

Guest speaker of several events: Mentone Event with Bill Bean, Mentone Event with Tiffany Johnson, Mentone Event Deborah Collard only, Alabama Paranormal Society Convention, ConNooga and many more.

Teacher of the Paranormal: Taught in Boaz, AL for one and half years, currently teaching in Mentone.

Paranormal Investigator Trainer: Trained numerous paranormal investigators across the state of Alabama & Georgia

Cold Case Remote Viewer and Psychic: Very private cases (Legal)

"Haunted Southern Nights®"

Volume 1

Ghost Hunting, the Basics+

Volume 2

The Haunted Backyard

Volume 3

History and Haunting of the Mentone Area

*History as researched and opinioned by D. Collard.

Volume 4 is coming soon!!!!!

www.ingramcontent.com/pod-product-compliance
Lightning Source LLC
Chambersburg PA
CBHW051759040426
42446CB00007B/447